RESOUNDING TRUTH

CHRIS BRAY

D1739073

The NIV translation has been used for all Biblical quotations throughout this book (except where specifically indicated).

I dedicate this book to the many patient, faithful, God-fearing friends who have shown me how to pursue truth through charity.

CONTENTS

PROLOGUE

I never wanted to write just another book with arguments and reasons to believe. There are already so many resources available, and they are far superior. Many of those books have been foundational in my faith life. However, I fear that our present culture is exchanging rational thought for individualism and relativism, and it may not be fully their fault.

Perhaps over the decades of evangelism, due to the failings of those who have abused such tools of apologetics, humanity has been treated less like God's beloved children, in need of a loving Father's gentle correction and illumination, and more like a pawn, sacrificed in pursuit of a trophy. Debates have moved away from an honest pursuit of truth, to pep rallies that boast a figure's egoistic pride.

With the rise and fall of social media, people have forgotten the dignity of the human person. We treat an opponent like we are going to war, even though we might refer to them as "friend", and all in the name of evangelization.

We might just be our own worst enemy, pushing away through malice, the very people we claim to be sharing the faith with. There must be a better way.

As a society, we have forgotten how to disagree well. What I mean is, that there was once an era when intellects would invite thinkers to ponder and reflect deeply on a subject. There was a time when understanding opposing viewpoints was necessary to accurately discern a subject matter.

Sadly, in today's culture of sound bites, if we suggest an alternate view, it is considered hate. Regretfully, in many cases, the actions of certain individuals have garnered that label. Perhaps people, myself included, have failed to communicate the truth with the utmost of charity. We've ostracized and vilified our opponents with egotistical condescension, rather than gentle persuasion.

In my own life, I've witnessed this done poorly. I've been the victim, and at times, regretfully, I've been the problem. To all of those numerous people, this is an apology.

I hope that this will not only serve as a resource to remove obstacles from those who are considering the truths of Catholicism, but even more especially, for Catholics desiring to grow in their appreciation for the faith and find a more effective way to lead people to the fullness of truth through charity and gentleness.

1

UPBRINGING

Some people are born with a gift or desire. In my case, the practice of apologetics was adopted out of necessity. God used certain paths and circumstances as opportunities for me to find a deeper faith life.

I grew up in a Catholic family. We did all of the right things. By that I mean, if we were devout Jews, we would have considered ourselves fulfilling the Law. We went to Mass every Sunday. We tithed. We memorized all the right prayers and responses. We even sang along to the best and the worst of the 1970s-era hymns.

We were a classic, token, legalistic, Catholic family. We had a deep-rooted sense of discipline. We fulfilled our obligation (which is often looked at only in the negative sense, but perhaps we should celebrate the good). The problem was, I'm not sure any of us in my family had a deep love for God. I was not in an authentic relationship with my Saviour. I didn't know who Jesus was.

Growing up I didn't need to know the "why" of my faith. I didn't understand why we had to go to Mass. I didn't know why the priest wore what appeared to be a toga. I didn't have the slightest clue why I needed to lunge (genuflect) when I would walk in. I knew about the Pope, and bishops, but didn't know what they did. In my mind, it seemed sort of like a ceremonious position, like the Royal Family of Britain. I knew the role was important but didn't know why. Perhaps meaningful ages ago, but I failed to understand its relevance and necessity today.

I knew words and phrases like Purgatory, the Immaculate Conception, penance, indulgences, etc. but if you were to ask me to describe them, I'd most certainly miss the mark.

I didn't know Jesus. I knew a little bit about what our faith taught, but not why. I think this is where many Catholics live for most of their faith life. They have a practice of faith (no matter how irregular) and this should be considered good, however, don't deeply know the love of God, and don't know the "why" of their faith.

I'm utterly convinced that if we as Catholics leaned into the "why", it would lead us closer and closer to the heart of God and enable us to fall in love with our Messiah. Likewise, if we knew God personally and had a burning desire for Him in our hearts, many of the theological obstacles that prevent people from pursuing the fullness of faith would simply fade away. I've witnessed this time and time again with new converts, stale Catholics, and adamant agnostics.

Thanks be to God, in my teen years I had a profound encounter with Christ. I began to know Him in a real way. This changed everything for me. I had a vibrant faith in Jesus, which was, for the first time in my life, alive. He was a real person to me, who knew me, loved me, died for me, and created me to be part of His will. I had the Spirit of God burning inside of me and truly felt born again.

Let us remember one important thing. Whatever the avenue of approach, union with God is the goal. If this is brought about through a compelling homily, praise God. If it's because of a time of personal prayer ministry, praise God. If it's brought about by way of private devotion, praise God. If it's inspired by a song of praise or hymn, praise God. If it's because of the encouragement and gentle leading of a friend, praise God. If it's because of the transmission of the gospel by way of book, audio or video, praise God!

Being in relationship with God, being in union with Him is, and must, always be the focus. All of the intellectual arguments and apologetics are meant to be in service of us falling in love with Him. If their use is not ordered that way, if they lack charity, then they have the possibility of having the opposite effect, being used as a weapon, or the very instrument that drives people away.

In retrospect, I realized that when I didn't know God, I also didn't understand the "why" of the faith. Perhaps if I did, I would have fallen in love with Him sooner. I also realized that when I knew Christ personally, I didn't have an immediate need to know the "why". This isn't necessarily a bad thing. There have been many Saints and faithful figures across the ages who were illiterate (St. Joan of Arc is a favourite example of mine), yet had a deep love for God. Academic knowledge of God is not a requirement for Heaven—thanks be to God!

It wasn't until later in my life that the "why" of my faith became important to answer. By pursuing the fullness of truth, I came to a much deeper faith in our Saviour, and a genuine love for His people.

2

MUSIC CAREER

Interestingly, God seemed to inspire in me, the very mechanism in which He drew me into relationship with Him. My initial drawing towards the faith was at a time in my life when I was struggling. Through an evening of prayer and worship through song, I came to know my Saviour. He wasn't just some ideology or worldview. He wasn't just a historical figure. For the first time in my life, I recognized that He was real.

When God opened my eyes to this discovery, I couldn't help but praise Him. That very night, we praised Him by praying. We praised Him by singing. We praised him on our knees in adoration.

I felt like God gave me a heart like David the psalmist. David would dance before the Ark of the Covenant. He would sing and write songs of praise to God for His goodness and His saving power. The Church of the ages adopted these songs (Psalms) which we still use to this day.

My heart began to burst with a desire to praise God this way. Thus, I was convinced God had a plan to birth a life of ministry ordered toward helping others do the same. I started writing my own version of David's praise Psalms. I began to help lead others to praise and worship God wholeheartedly. Somehow, God was starting to make a way, despite my inability. I was confident that this was the direction He wanted me to follow.

I remember quite vividly, one of the very first doors that were opened to the career I was zealous for. "We need a song for our youth conference, do you think you might be able to write one?". I remember getting off the phone with an event organizer gleaming with excitement. I was still in college and had aspirations of a career in Christian music. This was my chance to prove myself. I knew this Catholic youth conference well. I had attended as a teen participant. I helped the year prior as a young adult leader from the stage. I understood the theme, "We are called to love and serve".

I hung up the phone and grabbed my yellow notepad and a pencil. I started strumming, and humming and an hour later a song was born. So sure, and so confident this was going to be a fit, I sat down at my computer and started working on recording a demo.

I pressed on through the night, layering track after track of instrumentation between cups of coffee. The next day I laid down the vocal tracks and finally mixed it and pressed it to CD. I was full of excitement and hope. I even shared it with some family and friends and was pleasantly surprised when it was met with positive feedback. I remember thinking, "This is it. This is my chance".

I uploaded the song and sent an email to the organizer. Then I waited… Days turned into weeks. I just couldn't wait any longer so I called them up to see what they thought. They responded with, "Your song is nice". I don't like the word "nice", even to this day. It reminds me of how a grandmother would speak to a grandchild who drew a picture of an elephant with finger paint… "Unfortunately I just don't think it will be a good fit for us, but thanks anyway".

My dreams were crushed. This song was the embodiment of my hopes, squashed. My future aspirations seemed like a fairytale that was out of reach. How was God going to use me if I was simply a failure?

I put that CD on the shelf in a box and didn't open it for years. I forced myself to pack that part of my life away. "Yeah, I might do some music here and there", I thought, "but I guess I'm never going to *really* make it. My songs will just be for me and God".

It wasn't until years later when I was married that I felt God start to open doors and opportunities for me to pursue music in a new way. I was leading the music ministry in my home parish and doors were opening for me to lead at other events locally. I also felt a stirring to continue in songwriting and many new works were born.

A friend and mentor directed me to a music producer who had worked with many of the prominent Christian artists in Canada. We hit it off and agreed to work together. I was excited to get my songs recorded, but because of that early "rejection", I limited my dreams and expectations. I didn't think God had anything planned for that collection of songs beyond a "vanity" project.

As I continued to work with the producer, tweaking the songs and working towards a finished album, he sat me down and asked me a question, "Chris, I don't know if we have enough songs to make this album really 'complete'. Do you have any others?".

I had a bunch of "B" list songs in my notebook, but nothing I was prepared to share with him. "Not really", I said in response, with a sigh of discouragement. It was at this moment that I was reminded of the painful memory of that rejected song. It seemed like history was about to repeat itself. I worried if I'd even be able to put this album together. What if it wasn't any good? What if I got the first thousand CDs pressed and the only person who buys one is my mom?

I thought about it for a second and in a moment of grace, said to my producer, "Well, there is this one song I wrote a while back, but it's not very good". I pulled up the recording on his computer and we listened to the demo I recorded on my laptop back in college.

He said, "This is it!". This is exactly what we need. I looked at him in surprise. "Really?", I said, "Because it's not very good, in fact the conference I wrote it for didn't even want it, for free".

"No", he said, "This will be the first track on the album".

We re-recorded it the next week and suddenly the song came to life.

When we were getting close to finishing the album he sat me down again and asked, "Chris, have you thought about what you're going to do with these songs once the album is released?". "No", I responded, "I just assumed I would do what every other artist does... put some songs on the internet and play a 'gig' here and there".

My producer said, "I think you have some good songs here and I think you need to consider sending them to Christian radio for airplay".

I remember literally laughing out loud. "Are you kidding?", I said to him, "Why on earth would they want to play my songs?". "Trust me", he said confidently, and we got to work.

Fast forward a few months, and the very song that sat in the box on my shelf for years, the very song that was rejected, went #1 on the Canadian Christian radio CANCON chart and was blasting airwaves across Canada, and the world.

I remember the day when my wife and I were listening to Christian radio and I heard my song blaring, "We are called to live as Christ, we are called to evangelize, we are called to reconcile, we are called to love and serve the Lord today". I was stunned and in awe. Truthfully, I was actually in the shower. I heard my wife screaming from downstairs. I thought there was a mouse or large spider or something, so I ran downstairs sopping wet in a towel. We danced around the living room together in celebration of what God had done and I dripped water everywhere.

That song's milestone led to me being awarded "New Artist of the Year" at the Gospel Music Association Covenant Awards (among other accolades), which set in motion a new path God had in store.

It's hard for me to even share this story because I don't want to give the impression that I'm somehow boasting about what I've done or accomplished. I can tell you with all sincerity that this was God at work from beginning to end. If it were up to me, that song "Called" wouldn't have seen the light of day. It would still be locked in that box, a solace of protection from rejection and a painful reminder of my failure. Perhaps this is how many of us feel about sharing our faith with others. We lock our willingness to give a "defence of the hope that is in us" [1] away to protect ourselves from rejection.

But God took that rejection, that failure, and did something incredible with it. I can't claim any credit for it. It was all Him. I simply showed up (reluctantly). I'm so thankful to have been such a small instrument in His great plan. All glory to God!

That's what we are—instruments. God wants to use us and He is simply inviting us to be faithful. At first, it might seem like a failure. Perhaps in our interactions with others, we might even feel like the faith we are trying to share is being rejected. We must never lose heart. As long as we are faithful to God, and pursuing His path with love and trust, He can move mountains. We are instruments, just like apologetics is a tool. Like a skilled musician or seasoned sculptor who utilizes their tools of craft, we are to refine our gifts, relying on the tools of evangelism to produce the instrument's sound most effectively and proficiently.

This story, and so many more are constant reminders for me that God is at work all over the place. He's stirring in people's lives and circumstances, and most especially in our failures, inadequacies, and brokenness. He takes that "rejection" and redeems it.

It's precisely through all of these events and circumstances in our everyday ordinary lives that God invites us to be part of His plan. He works powerfully in these moments, not so we can lock them in a box, but so that we can share them with the world. Not to boast about our accomplishments, but to tell the world how incredible He is, despite our deficiency.

---

[1] 1 Peter 3:15

When we open our eyes to see the moments and opportunities God places before us, when we allow His Spirit and strength to overcome our fears and obstacles, and when we surrender to these opportunities of grace, not only are we giving Him glory, but He is using this as an opportunity to ignite faith in others!

I had a heart for praising God through prayer, worship and song. God was faithful and took what appeared as failure, and used it to demonstrate His power. Thrusting me into a full-time ministry was an amazing sight to witness and be part of. However, what He did next was both surprising and one of the most formative seasons in my life.

3

OPENED DOORS

One might assume because I was brought up in the Catholic faith and had a profound conversion to Christ in the Catholic Church that the ministry God was calling me to would be in that same arena. I know that I sure did. What I found interesting is that as my career in Christian music and full-time ministry was taking off, it wasn't Catholic Churches that were inviting me. It was Protestant communities.

At first, this seemed to surprise me. Why would these various denominations want me, a Catholic, to come to their churches? Furthermore, what seemed to hurt deeply was that the Catholic Churches showed no desire and no interest in me and my heart to inspire vibrant faith. I felt like an outcast in my own community. Once again, it felt like a rejection.

One of the main reasons that doors were opening in Protestant communities was because of Christian radio. Christian radio is run almost exclusively by various Christian denominations, sometimes even by a specific church itself. As a Catholic, writing songs of praise to God, there wasn't much of a platform for me in the Catholic world (unless I were to be writing hymn-style liturgical works). Though I had an appreciation for the polyphonic sacred hymns used in the liturgy, that wasn't the gifting God gave me, nor the desire to pursue. I wanted to help others experience and encounter God personally similar to how I encountered Him.

So trusting in God, and while receiving some scornful admonitions, I continued to pursue the path I felt God was leading me in. Because of the platform of Christian radio playing my songs, I began to receive invitations all over the country to come to various denominations.

I was amazed at what I experienced in contrast to what my faith was like growing up. I didn't see a legalistic faith, based merely on rules and obligations. I saw communities of people who actually desired to be together. I witnessed real relationships and friendships, people who cared that you were there. I saw Christians who had such a love for God, others, and serving, that they would come early to set up chairs, shovel snow and prepare for the worship service, without grumbling.

This is a stark contrast to what my Catholic community was like. Even the greeters at my home church wouldn't even look me in the eye or say, "Good morning", or look like they possessed the joy of the Lord. Many times the music minister would be chronically late and instead of being apologetic, would say with such attitude, "I'm here, I'm here, just give me a second…", like we should be grateful to wait for them, and their slightly less than prepared, highly resentful skill.

I fell in love with the idea that the church could be a community of people who were journeying together towards God. I loved that people actually had a desire to wait on the Lord and worship Him with all their hearts, minds, souls, and lives. I loved that I could clearly see God bringing people closer to Him, enabling them, by His grace, to surrender more deeply. I noticed this affection towards the Word of God. It wasn't just some ritualistic recitation, but a love letter from their Saviour inviting them to know Him more.

I'll be honest and say that I craved a real, authentic, sincere faith community to be part of, and sadly at that time in my life, I didn't see life within my Catholic community. However, I did come to realize later that there are pockets of communities like this in the Catholic world. I desired to be part of a church like in the second chapter of Acts, where people cared for one another. They had a deep and self-sacrificing love for God. They shared all things in common, cared for the poor and made sure no one lacked in anything.[2]

Why would I want to bring my kids to the Mass when it seemed like no one even wanted to be there? How can we create authentic community with people who don't have a common love for God, for others, and for serving Him? I felt both inspired and trapped.

My wife and I were very much tempted to "supplement" our faith with these non-denominational services, and I know in my heart that if we were to have travelled that path, it wouldn't have been long until we would have abandoned our Catholic faith altogether for a community that fed our soul and made us feel like we had life.

However, as I was wrestling with that struggle, I began to notice God doing something interesting. The more I travelled to non-Catholic churches for events, the more I began to see the best of what church should have always been like. I grew in this appreciation for a vibrant faith. But the people in those churches started to notice I was different.

----

2 Acts 2:42-27

I would perform a Christian concert or lead them in songs of praise and prayer to God. These events seemed to be powerful and fruitful. After the event or service, they would often ask me where I was from and what church I went to. This was where things began to get interesting.

For all they knew, I was just like them, an ordinary Christian with a love for God. But whenever I answered their question truthfully, "I live in a small little town, and I go to the Catholic Church", it seemed to be a startling revelation (especially when I said the actual name of our parish, which was a Marian title).

I can only imagine what some of them were thinking, though I don't want to judge. I noticed that they became very uncomfortable with the word "Catholic". It seemed to make them uneasy. Coming in innocently early on, I honestly wasn't too sure why. Growing up, I took my faith for granted. I didn't know the "why" of what we believed, nor did I have any comprehension of the schisms that have happened over the history of Christianity. On some level, I knew that other denominations believed slightly different things while having a large portion of the faith in common. In my mind, what I noticed was more differences in the outward expression of their faith and what they seemed to emphasize.

It didn't take long until I began to see there was a rift between Catholics and the rest of Christianity. They would often ask, "So then are you Christian or Catholic?". This seemed confusing to me. Of course, Catholics are Christians. It would be like if they were asking, "Are you Baptist or Christian...? Are you Lutheran or Christian...? Are you Pentecostal or Christian". Of course, they are all Christian. But for some reason, it seemed like "Catholics" were in a category all on their own. This became more and more apparent when I began to pick up on the confusing comments from people in the communities I was there to serve.

One evening after a worship event in a non-denominational church, upon finding out I was Catholic, a lady said, "Oh… well, we serve a living God, not a dead one". I was a little taken aback by it. Honestly, I didn't know how to respond, so I didn't say anything. Upon reflection later, I realized she was probably referring to the fact that we Catholics boast a crucifix (with Jesus on the cross still), while most other Christians simply have an empty cross (with a risen Christ).

On another occasion, immediately following the event, the pastor said to me, "Oh Catholic eh? You let some guy in Rome tell you what to believe?". I responded with a simple and slightly naive, "Yes…?".

Growing up Catholic, I didn't understand the "why" of my faith. I never really needed to, until those moments.

However, the Lord wasn't finished showing me what He was doing in my life. On another occasion, I had just released a brand new album and was excited to share these songs of praise with others in hopes that it would strengthen their faith and be able to be used as a tool to draw them closer to God. One of the songs I shared was called, "Seek The Things Above". The refrain has a line that says, "Don't let temptation, forfeit your salvation". Yes, I enjoy rhyming lyrics.

After the event, a lady came up to me and said, "I like your songs but I don't understand how you can suggest that temptation can possibly lead to you losing your salvation. Once you are saved, you can never lose your salvation". I had no idea what to say. All I could think was, "Ah, I think you can?".

But if she were to press me to show her how I wouldn't have even known where to start.

The more I travelled, the more questions I received that I had no idea how to answer. "Why did you Catholics add extra books to the Bible?". "Ummm, I don't know", is all I could muster up, having no idea what they were talking about. "Why do you worship Mary?", "Ahh, I don't think we do that", is all I could say and then quickly change the subject and hope they don't press the issue.

These people were well-meaning, but what I didn't quite fully understand yet, is that they had this caricature of what they understood Catholicism to teach. I don't believe many of them were being malicious or even putting it down in triumphalism. Honestly, I can understand their concern, if Catholics did worship Mary, that's a problem, right?

Finally, after months of these questions and feeling like a fraud in my Catholic identity, the nail on the coffin was this line in a conversation with a beautiful and well-meaning, non-Catholic Christian. When they asked about all the rituals, and ceremonial additives such as statues, vestments and candles, they said, "I get that we have a lot in common and that you love Jesus, but I just don't understand all that 'Catholic' stuff".

It hit me like a ton of bricks. I don't either. Part of me felt this overcompensation for wanting to prove these seemingly odd parts of Catholicism right for two reasons. First, because it was the faith of my youth, it was the faith in which I came to know Christ in a real way. If it was a fraud, did that mean that my faith in Jesus was also false? Secondly, and ashamedly, I wanted to prove Catholicism right out of spite and out of ego. I wanted to be right for the sake of winning. God forgive me, but

I have to be honest and admit that my intentions and motives weren't always pure.

Thankfully, despite all of that, God was patient with me. He took me on this incredible journey to discover this magnificent historical faith of the ages that goes back to the time of Christ and can be traced across history. It was not a moment-in-time conversion, but a long and hard journey of digging, learning and discovery.

4

ARCHAEOLOGY

After being bombarded with questions that I could never seem to answer, I decided that I needed to start learning the "why" of my Catholic faith. If I was ever going to help people understand how a Catholic could be so fired up for Jesus, I first would need to understand what we even believed and the reason behind it.

Muddled throughout was also a desire to not only answer these objections and questions but also prove them wrong. Reflecting on this season I realize how much damage that mentality did in fostering real ecumenical discussion. I feel like many discussions that take place today aren't really discussions at all. People come with agendas. People aren't necessarily interested in seeking after the fullness of truth but are more concerned with winning an argument. We listen to respond, not to understand.

I recognize this far too well because this was my struggle. It hurt my ego and pride when I didn't have a satisfactory answer. While this is an incredibly immature reason to want to share the faith in the name of "evangelism", God's mercy still used that opportunity to produce growth in me.

I am so thankful for those who were patient with me. I'm grateful for those who didn't give up on me, and journeyed with me, especially when I didn't deserve it, or when I failed to show them the charity and gentleness that they afforded me.

My application of the information wasn't always ideal or virtuous, but I was able to use that time I devoted to learning and understanding the "why", to reinforce the faith I professed to believe. Learning how to set my pride aside was something that took years of practice, and still requires constant effort for me to this day.

However, God used this information twofold. First, it empowered me to give meaningful answers and clarifications to people's misunderstandings of what Catholics believe. Second, it affirmed the truth of the Catholic faith in my life.

I had a moment where I decided to be committed to understanding the "why". Whenever someone asked me a question about the Catholic faith that I couldn't answer (which was mostly all of them), I would go and learn.

Part of this was because the questions themselves at times introduced doubt into my mind. I began to go on a quest to discover and unearth the truth. I would start researching online and reading what theologians had to say about any given topic. I wasn't satisfied with the sound bites and one-sided answers that I found, so I would keep digging.

In a lot of ways, I felt like an archeologist, digging into history, and unearthing new discoveries about our faith (which weren't really new, just new to me). Every time I would dig up a nugget of truth I felt like Indiana Jones. It became exciting. The more I dug the more I found. Suddenly, something that seemed like an empty ritual began to come to life, the more I realized the biblical and historical significance of it.

Something simple like incense is just one example. I never used to understand why we did it. It stunk up the church, it made the Mass take longer, and everyone would usually start coughing dramatically. I always used to think that it was just some ceremonious smoke, something we did because we've done it for a long time, and had nothing more than symbolic relevance today. But when I did a deep dive into Scripture, I found that incense embodies our prayers rising up to God (Revelation 8:4). It is an outward sign of a spiritual reality that was taking place right before me. In Revelation, when John got a glimpse of what is happening in Heaven right now, he saw incense rising up to God, containing the prayers of the saints (Revelation 5:8). Not only is incense continually being offered up to God with our prayers in Heaven as we speak, but God commanded from the beginning in the Old Covenant to offer incense to Him as part of our sacred worship (Exodus 30:1-10). And that just skims the surface.

Discovering one treasure at a time, and going deeper brought my faith to life. All of these seemingly unimportant aspects of our faith started to take shape. Everything from holy water, to candles, to the parts of the Mass, started to come alive. As I would partake in a particular liturgical posture or ritual, I began to vividly recognize that this is what was happening in Revelation, or this is how the early church operated in the book of Acts, not only in Scripture but also in the history and writings of the early church.

As the "why" continually started accumulating and stacking up, I was filled with zeal. One by one, my doubts about the historic Church of the ages were diminished. I felt empowered to be able to share this faith.

The more I began to learn, the more I realized that many of the objections were merely misunderstandings of what Catholicism actually taught. No, we don't worship Mary (for example), but I can understand how one might assume this based on observing a certain honour given to her, without understanding why.

It reminds me of how the first Christians were characterized by the pagan empire. Suetonius was a Roman secretary to Emperor Hadrian and wrote in The Twelve Caesars in the early Second Century, that Christians are "a class of men given to a new and mischievous superstition". [3] Numerous historical accounts at the time refer to Christians as "superstitious", "mischievous", "incestuous" and "cannibals".

When the empire heard how Christians stemmed from the rebel figure of Christ, considered a threat to the pagan empire, they were branded villains. Because Christians would gather for secret rituals, such as the Eucharist, in which only those baptized were allowed to partake, they were considered superstitious and secretive. Because they referred to one another as "brother" and "sister" (James 2:15) and were instructed to greet one another with a "holy kiss" (Romans 16:16), they were labelled incestuous. Because they claimed to consume the body and blood of our Lord Jesus Christ (1 Corinthians 11:24, John 6:53-56) they were referred to as cannibals.

Not much has changed in 1900 years. Today, due to misguided assumptions and misconceptions, either through innocent ignorance, perpetuated rhetoric, or something more sinister, Christians often misunderstand one another. Catholics in particular are given labels such as "idolaters" simply because

---

[3] Suetonius, a. 6. 1. (1957). *The twelve Caesars.*. [Harmondsworth, Middlesex], Penguin Books.

we have statues, and are called "goddess worshippers" because we give honour to Mary as the mother of our Lord.

What made my heart so happy was being empowered to clear away these misconceptions. It was never usually met with someone converting to Catholicism initially. But that wasn't my goal. I was simply trying to share a nugget of truth with someone who misunderstood what Catholicism taught, and why, and to try and do it gently with love. Ultimately, that's all we can do. The Holy Spirit does the rest. The Holy Spirit is the one who converts minds and hearts and draws us deeper into conversion and holiness.

The more pieces of the Catholic faith that I began to grab ahold of, the more I began to fall in love with God, His church and His plan for humanity all over again.

There were many times I failed along the way. There were many times I let my pride and ego lead, instead of prudence, patience, and charity. However, what I started to notice in my own personal growth, was that the moments and opportunities that God placed before me to witness and share my faith, when done so with love, were the most fruitful.

I believe God opened the doors of so many non-Catholic churches to take me on a journey. If I hadn't gone through that scrutiny I would not have the heart, zeal, and compassion towards those who struggle similarly. I wouldn't have gratitude and appreciation for what a vibrant, God-fearing, loving faith community should look like. I am very grateful to the many Christians who demonstrated what authentic faith is and how it can be lived out in our world.

What I found interesting, is that over time, those open doors became less and less, however, God started opening different doors—ones in the Catholic Church. I believe He was bringing me on that journey to prepare me, and to learn not only the "why" of the faith but how to effectively share it so that I can equip others to do so also. All of these melodies of discovery began to overlap into one resounding truth which led me into a deeper relationship with God and helped me to discover a new zeal and passion to share this truth with others.

5

ALWAYS BE READY

If there is only one chapter of this book you read, please let it be this one, and read it with an open heart. There is a famous passage of Scripture that apologists love to use as the banner for promulgating truth:

> " *But in your hearts revere Christ as Lord. Always be prepared to give an answer to everyone who asks you to give the reason for the hope that you have"*
> *(1 Peter 3:15-16).*

This is the rallying cry of the apologetic community. This is the bumper sticker Bible passage that gets applauded whenever a theological debate sparks.

However, what is often missed is the latter part of the verse which states, "…But do this with gentleness and respect". When was the last time we addressed our figurative adversary with reverence?

While it is important for us to be able to give a defence for the hope within us, to be able to share what it is we believe and why, what is equally as important is *how* we do this. Are we sharing out of love, charity, gentleness and reverence? Or are we sharing out of pride, ego, triumphalism, and maybe even malice?

This is what the effectiveness of our evangelization and apologetic efforts hinge on—respect and gentleness.

I understand this quite vividly from my own experience. It is very easy for us to be overcome with zeal and to get excited. Sometimes we have momentary lapses in virtue, where we need to reign in and drawback. What I've come to realize is that all of our efforts to share the faith must be pursued through the avenue of charity.

To quote Warren Wiersbe:

" *Truth without love is brutality, and love without truth is hypocrisy" (Warren Wiersbe).* [4]

Both must go hand in hand, yet many only focus on the facts and information. What I found time and time again, and what I witness constantly (especially on social media), is an overly confident, triumphalism, focused more on defeat than compassion for the other. This doesn't mean we are to diminish truth for the sake of another's feelings. It simply invites us to exercise wisdom, prudence and patience to be able to meet someone where they are, and journey along with them in pursuit of truth.

This is a compassion that walks alongside someone to help carry their load. It suffers with them in the obstacles that get in the way. It accompanies a person through the difficulties. However, most of Christian culture today is satisfied with writing them off as saying, "You're an idiot... but I'll pray for

---

[4] Warren W. Wiersbe (2011). "On Being a Leader for God", p.39, Baker Books

you", and we wonder why our evangelistic attempts aren't fruitful.

We've forgotten the patience of our Heavenly Father who slowly leads and guides us. He never gives up. He's slow to anger and rich in love. Instead, we've become comfortable vilifying others (sometimes even within our own religion) because of differing viewpoints. We are content with shutting down dialogue with phrases like, "You don't know what you're talking about", "You lost", and "See, I proved you wrong". As long as we end it with the words, "God bless, I'll pray for you", we're showing love, right?

This is not reverence and gentleness. This is punching someone in the face with truth, a form of evangelistic abuse, and then wondering why they won't stay for more. Why would anyone want to convert to be like that? For the fullness of truth to be compelling, it must demonstrate its superiority in virtue —a real transformation of the heart. A true and deep-rooted faith should be drawing us closer to holiness and virtue. The mistake we often make when pursuing apologetics in the name of evangelism is that we try and accomplish it void of charity. When that happens, all we are left with is brutality.

When I witness the petty bickering that happens online (and many times in person), I'm immediately turned off and disgusted. If non-Christians were watching, would that make them want to convert? Absolutely not!

Through my own faults and weaknesses in this arena, I had to devise a way to be able to share truth through love, a method which I will share shortly and is something I still use to this day.

One of the most compelling things I've witnessed is Christians who were confident in their faith, yet acted with the utmost of humility. One example is Francis Chan. He is an evangelical pastor whom I deeply respect. He is well known for his invigorating and inspiring sermons. However, there are two profound characteristics of this man that I appreciate immensely. First, he is oriented towards seeking after truth. He has a love for the Word of God and a desire to truly understand it. He often sets aside his predispositions and conclusions and allows the Word of God to be illumined in his life and his ministry. The second and most compelling aspect of this man that I admire is his demeanour, most especially his humility.

Chan is an accomplished missionary, speaker, author and megachurch pastor. He is well-known in the Christian community. He is deeply regarded and respected. But he is one of the most humble pastors I've ever encountered. Some might mistake humility for a lack of confidence. Don't misunderstand, Chan is confident (and knowledgable) in the Word of God and in his faith but has a rightly ordered humility. There is power in that virtue.

Imagine an opponent, whether a friend or pastor, who is so overly confident of theology, that they talk over you, shut down the discussion, and overload you with information, regardless of how well-intentioned. I have known zealous Catholics who do this mercilessly under the guise of evangelization.

Now picture someone who with the humility of Mother Teresa, embraces you, prays with and says, "Look, I don't have it all figured out myself, but I know God has the answers, and I want to journey with you on this together towards His truth, so let's begin…". This transcendental is what opens hearts, minds and ears to receive the fullness of truth more readily.

Time and time again, in my own failings, I've treated others poorly, lacking charity in my desire to win them over to truth. What has moved me the most was when I was less than charitable to another, and yet they had a patient love towards me. That resonated with me far more than whatever we were talking about. I am blessed to have numerous non-Catholic Christian friends in my life, some of whom are pastors of various denominations, who continually show me this humility. It is inspiring and has made for some of the best and most fruitful ecumenical bonding I've witnessed.

It's quite a contrast, isn't it? To go from name-calling to embracing a brother and praying in deep humility together. Theodore Roosevelt is known for saying, "People don't care how much you know until they know how much you care". [5] The avenue of our evangelistic and apologetic efforts must flow through the vain of love, gentleness and reverence. Even the most vile of contenders, God created, Christ died for, loves deeply and desires to obtain the fullness of truth and to be in authentic relationship with.

Because I've been blessed to have others demonstrate this patient gentleness and reverence, my method for sharing the faith is quite simple. Instead of using hostile and infuriating language, and instead of setting up traps or trying to slam dunk a conversation into submission, I try simply to imagine I'm speaking to those who were so gentle with me.

---

[5] Roosevelt, T. (n.d.). "People don't care how much you know until they know how much you care."

I ask myself, "How would I talk to this person if I was having this conversation with my beloved Protestant friend over coffee". That lens changes the tone of conversation immensely. How would Mother Teresa speak? Not what would she say, so much as *how* would she say it? The tone is how our gentleness and reverence are communicated.

Lastly, we need to remember that to journey with someone is a process. Consider for a moment a belief of your own that you hold so deeply. What would it take for you to reconsider that? We must constantly put ourselves in the shoes of those we are claiming to journey alongside. The word "compassion" is compounded from two Greek words: "passion" which means to "suffer" and "com" which means "with".

For a pastor to pursue theology that is not in line with their denomination would certainly mean losing their job, and risking financial ruin. I know we all like to think that would be an easy decision for us, after all, we simply follow God, right? But surely through the eyes of compassion, we can recognize the impediments and difficulty of pursuing that, especially with rashness and haste.

For a wife to leave a denomination that she and her husband have attended for their entire marriage would surely mean putting strain on the family and relationship. Which church would the children go to now? Both? Do they get to choose? Do they take turns? I'm sure the husband might mourn that he and his wife aren't in unity with what they once were.

One of the incredible stories I had the pleasure of hearing over coffee on one of my ministry journeys, was from BJ, a chaplain of a Catholic high school. I could tell right away that he had a profound love of God. He shared with me his journey to the Catholic faith from his Mennonite background. He wrestled with all of the same apologetic and theological arguments that most others do but coupled with all of that was his family dynamic. Leaving his Mennonite faith would mean rejection from his parents and friends. This is often a reality of the journey we can so easily dismiss or neglect to recognize.

It wasn't until BJ discovered a longing for the Eucharist that led him to pursue the Catholic faith. He found this beautiful mystery plainly situated in John 6 but was diminished and neglected by his prior denomination's tradition. He said that his church never read that part of Scripture where Jesus says, "Unless you eat my flesh and drink my blood, you will not have life in you… my flesh is true food, my blood is true drink" (John 6:53-55).

Finally, when he mustered up the courage to enrol in RCIA was met with an awful experience. Instead of finding a loving, and welcoming community, being sincerely interested in journeying with him and taking interest in what was drawing him to the Catholic faith, it was all business. BJ described the interaction as similar to legal proceedings. The coordinator was more concerned with ensuring the legalities of his baptism were performed correctly, and ticking off the requirements, than fostering and discipleship. It felt more like divorce proceedings than a welcome into the loving arms of a church that was waiting for him.

When BJ and his wife left that first meeting, they broke down and resolved to be done with Catholicism. Isn't that a sad reality? So many times as Catholics we get in our own way because we forget why we are doing this in the first place. It wasn't until six months later when BJ's wife was invited to another Catholic Church's RCIA program that things changed. Reluctantly she went, while BJ, though in full support of his wife, resolved to decline the offer. However, what she experienced changed everything.

She was met with a welcoming community of people, who wanted to know her, to hear her, to share in her journey and to understand where she was coming from. BJ relayed to me how, when she came home, she was filled with tears and said, "This is it. This is what we've been looking for". Finally, a community that understands that communicating the gospel with gentleness and reverence is as important as sharing the truth.

It's easy for us to drop a truth grenade and then walk away with judgements on their situation. It's a whole other thing to walk with them in this discovery and be with them through this struggle. That's what the journey is. Humility, gentleness, reverence and most especially charity, are the only things that will effectively enable us to lead others (and ourselves) to the fullness of truth in God. Facts, information and apologetics are only half of what it takes, and moreover, when used in isolation, are rarely effective.

So please, let us be ready to give a defence of the hope that is in us. Let us know so many of the reasons why we believe what we believe. Let us have a zeal and passion to quote Scripture, the Saints, the early Christian writings and even Church councils. However, let us always strive to deliver this with love, and be willing to follow up to journey alongside as we suffer with those we aim to love.

6

SEARCHING FOR HISTORICAL CHRISTIANITY

Having journeyed through the process of experiencing so many different denominations, and having witnessed so many different expressions of worship and faith practices, I was left with one question—*What did the first Christians believe?*

I had a new appreciation for communities of faith that were alive. I was so grateful to them for showing me what a living faith looks like. I was eternally grateful for how they fostered in me a love of God's Word. But still, I needed to know, with all the varying theologies and practices, what was true, and what God desired for His people.

Everywhere I went I saw communities that, while having so much in common, all seemed slightly different in what they emphasized. Some churches had a love for worship through song, others were more about proclaiming the Gospel in sermons. Some did communion regularly, while others only did it on special occasions, or not at all. Some had elders, some had overseers, some with female clergy, others rejected infant baptism... When I considered Christianity as a whole, I was left confused.

As I observed the vast array of Christianity, I couldn't help but wonder how the first Christians practiced. What did the early Christians believe? So many Christians today have such a heart and zeal for trying their best to align themselves with what Scripture says, and that should be applauded. Honestly, I wish as Catholics we paid more attention to conforming ourselves to the Word of God on the individual level. But I wanted to know what church was meant to look like, how we were meant to practice our faith, and what truth is.

This naturally led me to ponder, not only what Scripture says, but also those who lived it in the early days of Christianity. If I were a Christian in 75 A.D. (for example), what would that look like? How would I know what truth is? What did worship look like? What did the church look like? Was there a structure or blueprint?

I wanted to align myself with the true Christian church and the only way I could think to find that was to go right back to the beginning. Most people would suggest, the New Testament is the beginning. However, what I came to realize is that it is not.

Before there was a New Testament, there was the Church that Christ established. The books of the New Testament came later, much later. When I discovered the last book of the New Testament wasn't written until 96 A.D., I realized that Christianity had blossomed for sixty years before the Bible was finished being written. Not only that, but it wouldn't be for another couple hundred years until all of the books were promulgated, as they were geographically separated. It would be even longer to narrow down the several hundred manuscripts that were acclaimed as "scripture", to be declared the twenty-seven books of the New Testament that we have today. It would be another millennium after that until the compiled books of the Bible were readily available to any average Christian household (thanks to the technological advancement of the printing press).

So I asked myself if I were a Christian between 33 A.D. (when Christ died and rose) and 96 A.D. (when the last book of the New Testament was written), how would I know what truth is? What would my worship look like? What did the church look like? We see some of this described for us in the book of Acts. We get a glimpse and blueprint of the early church in minor regions. However, when I discovered the Church Fathers, I realized there was a whole testimony to what the historical Christian Church believed, that I was completely unaware of.

When most churches refer to church history, they tend to focus on the era between Jesus' birth and the death of the last Apostle, and then they fast forward until you get to the Reformation in the Sixteenth Century. Many Protestants earnestly believe that because of errors in theology and corruption within the Catholic Church at that time, that there was a need to break away and rediscover the *true* church. In a sense, this was the very journey I was on. I wanted to know the true church. I wanted to know what those first Christians really believed about God. I wanted to know the fullness of truth and align myself to it! I was so frustrated with churches drawing from the same book and interpreting the same Bible passages to mean different things. Surely, there had to be a way to know truth definitively.

The Church Fathers became my measuring rod, my lens to understand what Scripture meant. If there ever was a 'true' church, it must have been as close to the beginning as we could get. So that's what I dedicated myself to discovering. As I started to read what came immediately *after* the Bible era (the historical writings from the early Christians) I got a glimpse of what they believed, how they practiced and what they understood the Word of God to mean.

To be honest, it was shocking to me how so many Christians, from such an early time, could write so extensively on the faith. The early Church Fathers were prominent leaders in the Christian Church in the early centuries. They were the successors of the Apostles and many of them even learned from their feet. Surely if I was going to understand what true Christianity would look like, it was going to be from them. I wanted to get as close to the source as possible.

One of the things I realized quickly was that the biblical account of what Christianity looks like is quite small. It's easy to skew what little passages there are, to fit a certain modern mold. The incredible insight from the Church Fathers, and the unanimity on most matters, made it glaringly obvious what they believed, how they practiced, and how they understood the Word of God.

One of the first striking passages was from St. Ignatius of Antioch:

" *Let no man do anything connected with the Church without the bishop... Wherever the bishop shall appear, there let the multitude also be; even as, wherever Jesus Christ is, there is the Catholic Church" (St. Ignatius of Antioch).* [6]

---

[6] St. Ignatius of Antioch, Letter to the Smyrnaeans 8 (c. A.D. 110)

That is a bold and shocking statement. Within a decade of the last book of the New Testament being written, a bishop is claiming that the "Catholic Church" is Jesus' Church and that it is His very presence here on Earth.

Ignatius was ordained bishop under the instruction given by the Apostle Peter. He was also a friend and disciple of the Apostle John, learning from his feet. His letters were written on his way to martyrdom in Rome, to be eaten by lions at the Colosseum. This admonition is echoed over and over by others as well, helping to resolve my wondering—If I were a Christian before the New Testament was finished, how did I know what to do and believe? It seemed quite simple, Christ instituted a living Church (Matthew 16:18), not simply a book. Follow the Church, follow the bishop, and there we will find Jesus Christ.

This came with even more clarity when I started looking at the various heresies that arose in the early church. Things that we probably take for granted today, such as defining the Trinity (or in fact, creating an entirely new word which is not found in Scripture, to describe this reality). Or perhaps how the early church wrestled with Dyotheletism (that Christ had two wills, a human will and divine will) and so on.

Every time a prominent question about the faith or a heresy arose, which seemed to be out of line with the faith handed down from the Apostles, a council was called. These councils were made up of bishops from various regions, who were successors of the Apostles.

When I discovered this, it reminded me of the first council of Jerusalem. In Acts 15, we see a significant question arise in the church regarding salvation: do gentile believers in Christ, first need to be circumcised? So the presbyters of the church came together in a council to determine the matter. There are a few important considerations I noticed that might be worth pointing out.

First, while Christians at the time debated this issue, never does Scripture affirm it's up to each individual to figure it out for themselves. That point seemed quite clear and might sound almost offensive to many modern Christians today. I know it was offensive to me. After all, our fallen nature wants to be the one to decide what truth is in a culture of relativism.

Secondly, when the local Christians remained in disagreement, they appealed to two bishops: Paul (an Apostle) and Barnabas (also called an Apostle, but was appointed as a successor). Even they could not resolve this matter of grave importance alone. I found that compelling since it wasn't something that could be dictated or determined in isolation, even by an Apostle!

Thirdly, everyone agreed that this issue must be addressed and also agreed that the resolution was found by convening a council made up of Apostles, apostolic successors (men who were appointed as Apostles/bishops to take up their apostolic offices), and presbyters (often translated as "elders" in many Protestant translations).

This first council of Jerusalem, through the guidance of the Holy Spirit, proclaimed the doctrine that one does not need to be circumcised to be saved. This council then sent messengers to the surrounding churches so that everyone would know its decree (the Greek word used here is "dogmata", where the Catholic Church derives the word "dogma"), to be in unity in the faith, in theology and truth.

So here we see in the early church, an issue arose on what truth is. What I discovered is that the biblical model doesn't permit individuals to determine truth themselves. Similarly, there was no finished New Testament to appeal to for an authoritative decree. Before there was a finished Bible, they had a mechanism to know the faith, and operate. An authoritative council made up of Apostles and their successors (along with presbyters), guided by the Holy Spirit proclaimed a binding dogma on the universal church.

After discovering this blueprint, I progressed through history to the other major dilemmas found in the early church. In each case, a council was convened made up of bishops (the successors of the Apostles) to determine a decree through the guidance of the Holy Spirit.

It was like a lightbulb went off! This is how we can know truth. Christ established a Church, even before the Word of God was written, it was transmitted through His Church. Even when the Word of God was silent on an issue, it was the Church Christ established, through the guidance of the Holy Spirit, that would lead the faithful to the fullness of truth.

Across history, we have seen councils of apostolic successors convene to address the serious theological dilemmas of their time (Council of Nicaea in 325 A.D. on the nature of Christ; Council of Rome in 382 A.D. where we see the Canon of Scripture proclaimed... etc.).

This seemed so clear to me. This is how the Apostles operated in the New Testament, this is how the early church operated, even when the Bible wasn't finished being written and compiled. Surely, this is how Christ intended for the deposit of faith to be protected and promulgated across the ages.

Even more fascinating to me was that many of the Christians who discerned the Reformed position would reject certain proclamations from these councils, but would accept others. I couldn't quite understand why or how they could do this. How could someone trust that the Holy Spirit would guide the Church during a council and get one point correct (such as the Trinity or the Canon of Scripture), and during the same council get another decree wrong? Oddly enough, the twenty-seven books of the New Testament were dogmatically decreed (and subsequently affirmed) at these various early councils. How would a person know which parts of the council are correct and which are incorrect?

Most non-Catholic Christians today would hold in common that the Bible is the sole rule of faith. This came out of the Reformation in the Sixteenth Century. What I couldn't help but wonder was, how could the Bible be the sole rule of faith if before there ever was a written New Testament, there thrived a living Church?

Perhaps the answers I yearned for weren't found in finally cracking the right interpretation of a passage or hermeneutic gymnastic, but rather in leaning into the living organism of Tradition, which is the Church Christ founded.

The authority and structure of the early Church weren't the only noticeable attributes. Justin Martyr describes in detail what the Sunday worship liturgy was like:

" No one may share the Eucharist with us unless he
believes that what we teach is true, unless he is washed
in the regenerating waters of baptism for the remission of
his sins, and unless he lives in accordance with the
principles given us by Christ.

We do not consume the eucharistic bread and wine as if it
were ordinary food and drink, for we have been taught that
as Jesus Christ our Saviour became a man of flesh and
blood by the power of the Word of God, so also the food that
our flesh and blood assimilates for its nourishment becomes
the flesh and blood of the incarnate Jesus by the power of
his own words contained in the prayer of thanksgiving.

The Apostles, in their recollections, which are called gospels,
handed down to us what Jesus commanded them to do.
They tell us that he took bread, gave thanks and said: Do
this in memory of me. This is my body. In the same way he
took the cup, he gave thanks and said: This is my blood.
The Lord gave this command to them alone. Ever since then
we have constantly reminded one another of these things.
The rich among us help the poor and we are always united.
For all that we receive we praise the Creator of the universe
through his Son Jesus Christ and through the Holy Spirit.

On Sunday we have a common assembly of all our
members, whether they live in the city or the outlying
districts. The recollections of the Apostles or the writings of
the prophets are read, as long as there is time. When the
reader has finished, the president of the assembly speaks to

us; he urges everyone to imitate the examples of virtue we have heard in the readings. Then we all stand up together and pray.

On the conclusion of our prayer, bread and wine and water are brought forward. The president offers prayers and gives thanks to the best of his ability, and the people give assent by saying, "Amen". The eucharist is distributed, everyone present communicates, and the deacons take it to those who are absent.

The wealthy, if they wish, may make a contribution, and they themselves decide the amount. The collection is placed in the custody of the president [presider], who uses it to help the orphans and widows and all who for any reason are in distress, whether because they are sick, in prison, or away from home. In a word, he takes care of all who are in need.

We hold our common assembly on Sunday because it is the first day of the week, the day on which God put darkness and chaos to flight and created the world, and because on that same day our saviour Jesus Christ rose from the dead. For he was crucified on Friday and on Sunday he appeared to his Apostles and disciples and taught them the things that we have passed on for your consideration" (St. Justin Martyr). [7]

---

[7] St. Justin Martyr, First Apology 66 (A.D. 151)

When I read this passage I was shocked. Justin Martyr described the exact format of the Mass I had reluctantly celebrated my entire life, except it wasn't some recent adaptation. This was documenting the orthodox practice of Christians within a generation of the last book of the New Testament being written. While I had been so unsatisfied with the exteriors (the music, the preaching, the miserable people), the early church assembled gladly for something beyond the superficial. They were almost unanimously zealous that the bread and wine in the Eucharist was the "flesh of our Savior Jesus Christ, flesh that suffered for our sins and that the Father, in his goodness, raised up again", in the words of St. Ignatius of Antioch. [8]

The Mass was the real presence of Jesus, not just a symbol, not just spiritual, but in the same sense of His physical presence dying on the cross. If someone were to have lived when St. Ignatius wrote that letter, in the same era as when the book of Revelation was penned and dared to suggest otherwise, then they were a heretic from the one true faith.

In my own selfishness, I was rooting for the Catholic Church to finally get with the times. Adopt rock music, and make it more appealing, less boring, and more inspiring. However, what I didn't realize is that the same Mass celebrated today in Catholic Churches around the world, has been left essentially unchanged for two thousand years. I realized that perhaps it wasn't the Church that needed to change, but rather my own heart of stone.

---

[8] St. Ignatius of Antioch, Letter to the Smyrnaeans 6–7 (A.D. 110)

Now it's important and necessary to point out that the writings of the Church Fathers serve us merely as a historical glimpse into what they believed. These writings are not inspired. They are not inerrant. Their writings are not Scripture. Some of them erred individually. Some of their writings contain heretical errors (even by the standard of the Catholic Church). Because as individuals they were not perfect, and were not infallible. However, as a whole what we get is a clear picture as to what early Christianity looked like, what they believed, and how they practiced.

The more I kept reading them, the more I saw clear lines and distinctions as to what the first Christians truly believed. Baptismal regeneration, confession, penance, apostolic tradition, intercession of the saints... all of these defining attributes pointed to only one of two possibilities. The faith of the early Christians was only found today in either the Roman Catholic Church or Eastern Orthodoxy (and for the first millennium those two were one and the same). These are the only two Christian branches that remotely echoed the early Church Fathers. There was one determinant that made the choice quite simple—the Office of Peter and the Keys of Kingdom.

Now I want to invite you to pause for a moment. I've just condensed about five years of my life's journey through apologetics in a few short and brief paragraphs. Someone reading this might see me jumping to these conclusions and suggest that I did so irrationally and without cause. Let me assure you, that this is simply the overview of the journey and we will dive deep into the struggle of each of these hot-button issues one by one.

I was earnestly wrestling with the dilemma that if the church held all of these beliefs in common, many of them almost unanimously, for an entire millennium, right from the end of the First Century, how could the Reformation have rejected them so easily? The more I tried to find the five solas of the Reformation in the early Church, the more I recognized their absence (at least on the points where they differ from Catholicism).

Now, I want to be fair because even among various denominations, Reformers seem to articulate what each of the five solas means in their context with a delicate nuance. It's hard to address a vast array of understandings with a generalization and one brush stroke. However, what was clear to me is that the Church Fathers seemed Catholic and I couldn't seem to find much Reformed theology in the early Church.

One surprising practice that I noticed throughout the numerous discussions I had engaged in with many friends and pastors who come from the Reformed perspective, is that they would often try to appeal to early Church writings for support. While some Church Fathers use vague language in certain areas, such as saved "by faith", and even "faith alone" (for example), what I found is that the same Church Father, oftentimes even in the same letter, would write affirming the orthodox teaching, rather than the Reformed position. However, these quotes contrasted with the Catholic view, were overwhelmingly outnumbered and disproportionate.

Jesus promised us that the gates of Hell would not prevail against His Church. This means there will never be a time, when His Church is overcome, and corrupt. It means that not one iota, not one command of His shall pass away or be forgotten. This means that there will always be a living Church to hand on the fullness of the true faith across the ages. It will never expire, never pass away, never be wiped out. Christ's Church will never be apostate. The Church Fathers showed me how this was possible before there even was a Bible.

Again, the Church Fathers aren't Scripture. It's not all gold. They aren't inerrant. But I realized that if you were to try and get a sense of what the early Church believed, apart from cherry-picking certain verses, you'd find a clear answer in their writings. Trying to discover the essence of Christian life through the lens of the Church Fathers, paints a vivid image.

I don't want to come across as overbearing. I can understand how someone from another perspective could quite easily read this part of my journey and feel put off by the assertions I'm making. I realize that many people who are much more intelligent than I, have read the Fathers of the Church and have not come to the same conclusion. However, I also feel that this is not so much a test of intelligence, but rather of our willingness to allow the Lord to open our eyes of faith to see the history of Christianity apart from the predispositions we've been taught through. If this line of thinking and my journey of searching for the true historic Christian Church is making you uncomfortable, and if this is as far as you read, I'll ask you to do one final task. Please, don't take my word for it. If you read nothing else, no other apologetic arguments for the faith, please simply start reading the early Church Fathers. All of their writings are available for free on the Internet and through print media. Stop listening to me, and go read their writings. Read what the first Christians did, what they believed, and how they practiced. If nothing else, you will be inspired by those Christians, most of whom were martyred and put to death for what they professed to believe.

Once I discovered this, the only thing I could consider was that if this is how the first Christians practiced and this is what they believed—how could I not do the same and follow suit?

7

THE BIBLE ALONE

The foremost obstacle I found in my search for the fullness of truth was the interpretation of Scripture. I want to suggest that this individuality of the interpretation of Scripture might be the foremost culprit for division in the Christian Church today.

Every new church I visited seemed to have a slightly different take on a passage. Some people would stack certain verses together, appearing to lean towards one theology. Others would stack other verses together coming to the opposite conclusion. Not only did denominations evolve with their identity marked in these distinctions, but now even within these denominations, individuals would take these interpretive liberties even further (including Catholics). I struggled to see the merit in a system that relies on interpretive superiority as an individual, to be able to know truth, especially in light of Peter's admonitions:

" *Above all, you must understand that no prophecy of Scripture came about by [one's] own interpretation of things" (2 Peter 1:20).*

And he went on to say:

" *[Paul's] letters contain some things that are hard to understand, which ignorant and unstable people distort, as they do the other Scriptures, to their own destruction" (2 Peter 3:16).*

As I looked around the Christian community, the common thread to this issue seemed to be "sola scriptura" or the notion that the Bible alone is the sole rule of faith. It was the anthem of the Reformers.

This discussion is probably the one I've pursued the most out of every piece of theology debated. To be fair, there are varying degrees of belief on this subject. But from what I can generalize, the widely accepted understanding among those who hold to Reformed theology is this:

" *The Bible is the sole infallible source of authority for Christian faith and practice".* [9]

To be honest, I can see why this would seem compelling. Especially at the time of the Reformation, when individual clergy were abusing power and skewing theology for personal gain. In a world of corruption, it might seem like the only sure way to know truth is in the written Scriptures.

I definitely understand why so many people could agree with the Bible as the only and final authority. After all, with human error and flaws, what else could be reliable as the final

---

[9] Wisse, M. (2017). PART I: Systematic Perspectives – Contra et Pro Sola Scriptura. In H. Burger, A. Huijgen, & E. Peels (Eds.), *Sola Scriptura: Biblical and Theological Perspectives on Scripture, Authority, and Hermeneutics* (Studies in Reformed Theology, Vol. 32, pp. 19–37). Leiden: Brill Publishers.

authority? In all sincerity, I wish Christians today (myself included) more closely followed the Bible, and applied it to their lives.

However, the reality is that Christians don't disagree on what the Bible says (for the most part), but rather what it means. This circles back to the issue of interpretation. What frustrated my journey towards the fullness of truth was all of these denominations claimed to follow the Bible alone as their only and sole authority, and yet they all disagreed on what it meant. They all had some form of opposing theology and all used the same book as their rule of faith. When I looked around Christian culture, I just saw a mess of dysfunction, and everyone claiming to be "biblical". So I decided to take this issue to the Scriptures to see if there was merit to this supposition.

The first passage that stood out to me was Matthew 18:15-18. If an issue arises, Christ instructs us to approach our brother first. If they don't listen, then take two or three witnesses. If they still don't listen, it says to finally "take it to the church" (Matthew 18:17), and if they don't listen "even to the church", they are like outcasts. The church is the final authority to resolve matters. This is echoed again in the first council of Jerusalem (Acts 15).

So I pondered if the Bible actually claims to be the sole and only rule of faith and final authority. One of the passages most appealed to on this matter is from 2 Timothy 3:

“ But as for you, continue in what you have learned and have become convinced of, because you know those from whom you learned it, and how from infancy you have

known the Holy Scriptures, which are able to make you
wise for salvation through faith in Christ Jesus. All
Scripture is God-breathed and is useful for teaching,
rebuking, correcting and training in righteousness, so that
the servant of God may be thoroughly equipped for every
good work" (2 Timothy 3:14–17).

Firstly, there is so much to be appreciated about this passage. "All Scripture" is God-breathed. All Scripture is His Word. Amen! So let us lend an ear to His Word. Secondly, Paul states here that Scripture is profitable for teaching, reproof, correction, and training in righteousness. Amen again! Let us rejoice to have such a gift to be transformed towards holiness and service. Lastly, this passage states that it is so a man of God *may* be complete and equipped for good works.

When I wrestled with this passage I got stuck on one crucial question—is one brought to completion by *Scripture* or by being *reproved*? I was able to realize the beauty of this passage with an analogy. Suppose I bought a book because I wanted to learn how to get fit. The book had everything I needed to know about how to weight train, and how to eat to grow muscles and lose fat. It had the workout routines and taught me how to do the exercises. It overviewed nutrition, explained how to track macros and even provided recipes. It contained everything that I needed. It was all in that book. But if I didn't do the things it told me to do, and I didn't follow the training, would my fitness transformation be brought to completion? No.

As Christians, we have to participate and do the training. We have to go through to process of being reproved and corrected. Just having the book to tell you how to be reproved and corrected isn't enough. We have to apply it. It's through applying the training, by being reproved, by being corrected, that the servant of God "may" be (not guaranteed, but aiming to be) brought to completion and is "equipped for every good work". What is profitable (as Scripture states) for this transformation to happen? Scripture. All Scripture is helpful for this training, so that man may be brought to completion and equipped.

When I went back and re-read this passage from Paul, I wasn't able to get on board with the idea that Scripture somehow claims to be the sole and only rule of faith. It's profitable, yes. Does it claim to be the absolute and only? Not in this passage.

Now something else interesting to point out is if Christians are going to take this passage in an absolute sense, we have a bigger problem. As Paul states to Timothy, "...continue in what you have learned and have become convinced of, because you know those from whom you learned it, and how from infancy you have known the Holy Scriptures, which are able to make you wise for salvation through faith in Christ Jesus". I must have read this passage a thousand times before someone pointed this out to me. The only "Holy Scriptures" that would have existed to make Timothy "wise for salvation", that Paul was referring to, is the Old Testament. If we are going to take this passage to mean that Paul in an absolute and explicit sense, means that Scripture alone completes a servant of God, then it goes too far. What he would be saying is that the Old Testament alone is all sufficient, and the sole infallible rule of faith for Christians! To clarify, I don't believe this, and I've never met any other Christian who does either. However, to read this passage in the absolute sense (as those who extrapolate sola scriptura from it do) forces us to arrive at this logical conclusion.

Perhaps an easier approach is to ask what the Word of God is. Ultimately, the answer is Jesus. At the beginning of the Gospel of John, we are reminded of this reality, "In the beginning was the Word, and the Word was with God, and the Word was God…The Word became flesh and made his dwelling among us" (John 1:1, 14). Christ, the Word, came to us in the flesh. He spoke His word across the ages through Moses and Elijah, through the Law and Prophets. He gave us His Word while He walked the Earth and spoke. Some of this was recorded in writing (this is what we have accounted for in the New Testament), but the Word of God He spoke was not all written in Scripture. At the end of John's Gospel he states, "Jesus did many other things as well. If every one of them were written down, I suppose that even the whole world would not have room for the books that would be written" (John 21:25). John emphatically drives home the eternalness of the Word of God. Jesus always existed, and even the things He said and did could not be contained in all of the books in the world. When I came across this passage it dawned on me that of course, not everything Jesus said and did was recorded in the Scriptures. He did other things also. And those other things He said and did were equally as much the Word of God.

I started to wonder if there were any examples of the Word of God being taught, which weren't recorded in Scripture. One particular example that struck me was when Jesus was speaking to the Scribes and Pharisees in Matthew 23:

> *" The teachers of the law and the Pharisees sit in Moses' seat. So you must be careful to do everything they tell you. But do not do what they do, for they do not practice what they preach. They tie up heavy, cumbersome loads and put them on other people's shoulders, but they themselves are not willing to lift a finger to move them" (Matthew 23:2-4).*

"Moses' seat" is a chair of authority and judgement (Exodus 18:13) over the people of God. Jesus is now affirming (in Matthew 23) that the Scribes and Pharisees now sit in Moses' seat. Jesus affirms that they have the authority to bind the Law. What I found fascinating is that nowhere in the Old Testament do we see them being appointed or adopting this authority. Yet, Jesus affirms they have it, and the faithful of God must listen to their authority.

To me, that seemed like a pretty big deal. That's almost as audacious as the Pope claiming to have authority over the Church (please read that with some tongue and cheek). However, right here in the Gospel of Matthew, we have an example of the Word of God, not recorded in the Sacred Scriptures of the Old Testament, yet affirmed by Christ Himself as true. This opened my mind to what the Word of God is. God's Word is not limited to merely what was eventually written down in the Scriptures.

Scholars and historians suggest that the book of Genesis wasn't finished being written for almost a millennium (or at least centuries after Moses lived). [10] Think about that for a moment. The Word of God as given to Moses, was proclaimed and carried orally for hundreds of years before it was documented in Scripture. However, before its dictation, it was still just as much the Word of God as in its written form.

I started to pursue this concept even more as I explored the New Testament. I began to wonder if Scripture affirms this notion that the Word of God is not limited to the text on the written page, but also what was proclaimed orally. Paul makes this clear:

> *And we also thank God continually because, when you received the word of God, which you heard from us, you accepted it not as a human word, but as it actually is, the word of God" (1 Thessalonians. 2:13).*

He goes on to say:

> *So then, brothers and sisters, stand firm and hold fast to the teachings we passed on to you, whether by word of mouth or by letter" (2 Thessalonians 2:15).*

By this point, it seemed quite clear to me that even the Apostle Paul recognized that the "Word of God" was just as authoritative when delivered by "word of mouth" or taught through "traditions". At this point in my journey, I came to understand that the Word of God exists in two forms, first, as Sacred Tradition (oral transmission, the Word of God handed

---

[10] Van Seters, J. (1998). The Pentateuch. In S. L. McKenzie & M. P. Graham (Eds.), *The Hebrew Bible Today: An Introduction to Critical Issues*. Westminster John Knox Press.

down and spoken) and as Sacred Scripture (the Word of God which was eventually written down).

I can understand the struggle many modern Christians would have to adopt Sacred Tradition as the Word of God. After all, generations of us have known a world with information available at our fingertips and with libraries full of books. What might be helpful to remember is that for most of salvation history, this wasn't the case. It's only in the last few hundred years that each Christian having access to the Sacred Writings was common. Imagine living in the Old Testament and having no access to a written form of the Law (because it hadn't been written down yet). Imagine living in the First Century before the New Testament was even written. All you would have is the oral transmission of the Word of God, which is the Sacred Tradition handed down through the ages. Yet, for the church, it was just as authoritative as what came later in the Sacred Writings.

What I came to appreciate later on in my journey, was a document the Catholic Church produced entitled Dei Verbum (Second Vatican Council, 1965), which helps to better understand the relationship between Sacred Scripture, Sacred Tradition and the role of the Magisterium in upholding the Word of God. [11] It echos what Paul wrote in 1 Timothy 3:

> *If I am delayed, you will know how people ought to conduct themselves in God's household, which is the church of the living God, the pillar and foundation of the truth" (1 Timothy 3:15).*

---

[11] Second Vatican Council. (1965). *Dei Verbum.*

I'd highly recommend taking a moment to read and appreciate how beautifully and eloquently the document Dei Verbum illuminates how Christ, the Word, has given us the Word, and instituted a living Church to uphold it.

My Reformed friends would often cite Paul praising the Berean Jews who were more "noble-minded" than the Thessalonians for searching the Scriptures eagerly to test that the revelation Paul was giving them was true (Acts 17). Many suggest this is a prime example of sola scriptura at work. The question to ask is, why are the Bereans more noble-minded than the Thessalonians? The Thessalonians ultimately rejected what Paul had to say. They compared Paul's message to the Old Testament Scriptures and decided he was wrong. Which group seems closer to sola scriptura? The Bereans who accepted new revelation from Paul orally, and sought further understanding from the Word of God, or the Thessalonians who rejected this new revelation because they couldn't see it in the Scriptures alone?

After all of this consideration, and even without hearing from the Church Fathers on this issue, it became apparent to me that the Scriptures never claimed to be the sole and only rule of faith for God's people. How could it? When for much of history, the Word of God wasn't even recorded in the Scriptures.

Now if there was one consideration that made the concept of sola scriptura, and going by the Bible alone, an impossible and illogical theology to accept, it was the Canon of Scripture. The Canon is the list of books that make up the Bible. We will dig into the apologetics for the Canon itself later in this book.

However, it was knowing the Canon, specifically of the New Testament, that made utilizing Scripture alone an unreasonable option.

In one of my many discussions on this subject with a beloved Protestant minister, I asked him if everything he believed came only from the Bible alone. I appreciated his honesty when he replied that he strives to follow only the Scriptures and that he is careful to not add to it, or remove from it. I commended this, as I wish we as Christians would yield to the Word of God more carefully.

However, I asked him quite frankly, "If you go only by the Bible alone as your ultimate authority, how do you know which books make up the Bible?".

He was very gracious with his answer and spent a great deal of time talking about the history of the Old Testament, and how some of the Epistles were written by Apostles. But again I asked him, "But where do you find the doctrine of the Canon (which books make up the New Testament) in the Bible". This seemed to put a pause in his thinking.

It seemed like the more I asked for him to point out a passage or verse that gives us the doctrine of the Canon, the more he appealed to how the Apostles handed down these books throughout history. He shared how the early Christians would weigh the contents of a particular writing against the tradition handed down from the Apostles.

I agreed with him, that of the 200-300 early writings claiming to be inspired and used as Scripture, somehow the New Testament was narrowed down to 27 books. They knew what wasn't Scripture because they had something to compare it against (Sacred Tradition).

But then I pointed out that when I asked him to show me where in the Bible the teaching of the Canon was found, he had spent his time appealing to history and tradition, something other than the Bible. I understand the difficulty of this task, and that as Christians we often take this for granted, but still the question was left open.

So instead of having to prove the entire New Testament teaching of the Canon, I asked him if he could demonstrate, from the Bible alone, why even just one book, the book of Hebrews (as one example), should be included. As you can imagine, this is an impossible task.

Scholars don't know definitively who wrote the book of Hebrews. We don't have the original manuscript to prove authenticity. Nowhere does that letter claim inspiration or to be Scripture. No other writing of Scripture claims that Hebrews is inspired. So why is this included in the Canon (especially if there is no biblical evidence to include it)? How can a Christian who adopts sola scriptura even believe in the Canon of the New Testament, if there is no Scriptural evidence to support it? Is that not a self-refuting ideology?

The more I pondered this dilemma, the more obvious this glaring issue became. If the Bible doesn't say which books make up the Bible, then, by the very logic of sola scriptura, we must reject what is not found in Scripture. That would mean rejecting almost the entire New Testament. As I'm sure you would agree, this would be utter nonsense.

What I realized is that everyone who adopts the belief of going by the Bible alone as the ultimate authority is ironically not going by the Bible alone. Every attempt to prove the Canon of Scripture (arguably one of the most essential Christian teachings), appealed to something other than the Bible (usually history and tradition). The irony was very striking.

One of the charges often laid against this criticism is falsely articulating sola scriptura as "solo" scriptura. Many proponents of this teaching would suggest that they still lean on tradition and history, however, they place the authority of the written Scriptures above those. I can appreciate that. The problem that I found is that on a practical level, this is rarely the case. Whether it was something like Purgatory, the Papacy, or the Immaculate Conception, Reformers would hastily reject those teachings (even though there is biblical evidence of support), all the while accepting other essential teachings (such as the doctrine of the Canon) with no biblical evidence. It seemed to me like the "extra-biblical" doctrines they wanted to accept (such as the Canon), they would choose to do so even if it meant diminishing or ignoring sola scriptura, but as soon as there was a purported "extra-biblical" distinctively Catholic teaching (such as the Papacy, which has significant biblical evidence), they would reject it under the banner of sola scriptura. I began to be frustrated with the inconsistency and ambiguousness of this practice.

I found that the more I tried to convey this dilemma, the more pushback I would get. Many of those who promote this teaching as the best way for the church to operate, would often ask what essential teachings are absent from Scripture, that are so important we would need something other than the Bible.

Apart from the Canon itself not being found in Scripture (which personally I think is quite essential and foundational), I started digging to see what some of the other important

Christian doctrines are, that are widely held but aren't found in the written Word of God.

Are there any teachings that practitioners of the Bible alone follow, that are not found in the Bible? What I found was a surprising list:

" **Dyotheletism** — *Dyotheletism is the doctrine that Christ has two wills, one human and one divine. This is not explicitly found in Scripture, however, is widely accepted by Christians. It was dogmatically decreed in response to the heresy of Monothelitism, by Pope Agatho in his dogmatic epistle (Sixth ecumenical council, Constantinople III in 681).*

" **A List of Essential Teachings** — *Whenever I challenged the notion of sola scriptura, and most especially the issue of there being a plethora of biblical interpretations, I was usually told that Christians, "agree on the essentials". If that is the case, it would seem that there would be a list of essential teachings found somewhere in Scripture, that Christians would agree on. However, Scripture doesn't seem to outline this list, and what I found more perplexing is what those essential teachings even are, which many Christians don't agree on.*

" **The Bible Interprets Itself** — *Whenever I would show concern for how we might be able to correctly interpret the Sacred Writings, and how we can be sure our interpretation is correct, many proponents of sola scriptura would suggest that the Bible interprets itself. There is a* *study of biblical interpretation known as hermeneutics. However, Scripture is written text. Written text can't interpret other written text. When I first encountered this I couldn't help but compare it to saying something along the lines of, "A book can read itself". We can apply historical contexts to try and better understand the significance. We can compare how certain Greek words are used in other places to try and garner some insight as to what they mean. We can even overlap other passages to try and seek an understanding. But a book can't interpret itself. In Matthew 13:24-30, Jesus shares a parable of the wheat and weeds. Peter later appeals to Jesus to explain what these words mean. They didn't explain themselves.*

" ***The Ceasing of Public Revelation*** *— There is a common understanding among Christians that public revelation ceased with the death of the last Apostle. However, as I looked for a way to prove this from Scripture, I couldn't find a passage that states this to be true, or prophesies that this would happen. The fact that it's widely held is a testament to the reality that we rely on tradition, and something other than the Bible alone, to believe this teaching.*

" ***The Trinity & Hypostatic Union*** *— These are words that were invented to describe their respective realities. Some bits and pieces point to both of these teachings found in Scripture. While these realities are alluded to partially in the Bible, these dogmas are not articulated explicitly. In fact, one of the reasons Christians wrestled with the heresies* *surrounding these two issues is because Scripture isn't obvious about them.*

There are more examples as well, but by this point, once I started cataloguing all of the things that we believe as Christians and can't know from the Bible alone, it seemed compelling to me that this doctrine was both unreasonable and self-refuting.

My last litmus test was to investigate what the early church believed regarding the Word of God, and if they taught that the written Scriptures alone were the ultimate authority.

In the Second Century, St. Irenaeus of Lyons wrote:

❝ *Since therefore we have such proofs, it is not necessary to seek the truth from others that is easy to obtain from the Church; since the Apostles, like a rich man [depositing his money] in a bank, lodged in her hands most copiously all things pertaining to the truth: so that every man who will can draw from her the water of life. For she is the entrance to life; all others are thieves and robbers. On this account we are bound to avoid them, but to choose the thing pertaining to the Church with the utmost diligence, and to lay hold of the Tradition of the truth. For how stands the case? Suppose there arises a dispute relative to some important question among us, should we not have recourse to the most ancient churches with which the Apostles held constant intercourse, and learn from them what is certain and clear regarding the present question? For how should it be if the Apostles themselves had not left us writings? Would it not be necessary to follow the course of the Tradition that they handed down to those to whom they committed the churches?" (St. Irenaeus of Lyons)* [12]

The early Christians understood as Irenaeus states, that "all things pertaining to the truth" can be found in the Church.

In my quest to test the early Church Fathers, to see if they practiced the concept of sola scriptura, I appealed to their writings. At first, it seemed as though some of them did suggest that the Scriptures were the final authority. Many of them affirmed the Sacred Writings to be appealed to. I even carefully catalogued several quotes from the Fathers, that when read in isolation, appeared to suggest they might have believed it too.

A few examples include quotes from Irenaeus, Tertullian and Hippolytus:

" *We have learned from none others the plan of our salvation, than from those through whom the Gospel has come down to us, which they did at one time proclaim in public, and, at a later period, by the will of God, handed down to us in the Scriptures, to be the ground and pillar of our faith" (Irenaeus of Lyons).* [13]

" *It will be your duty, however, to adduce your proofs out of the Scriptures as plainly as we do, when we prove that He made His Word a Son to Himself. . . . All the Scriptures attest the clear existence of, and distinction in (the Persons*

[12] St. Irenaeus of Lyons, Against Heresies. (A.D. 189). Book 1, Chapter 10, Section 2

[13] Irenaeus of Lyons, Against Heresies, 3.1.1, A.D. 202

*of) the Trinity, and indeed furnish us with our Rule of faith"
(Tertullian of Carthage).* [14]

❝ *There is, brethren, one God, the knowledge of whom we
gain from the Holy Scriptures, and from no other source.
For just as a man if he wishes to be skilled in the wisdom of
this world will find himself unable to get at it in any other
way than by mastering the dogmas of philosophers, so all of
us who wish to practice piety will be unable to learn its
practice from any quarter than the oracles of God.
Whatever things then the Holy Scriptures declare, at these
let us look; and whatsoever things they teach these let us
learn" (Hippolytus).* [15]

Upon reading these, and many other excerpts, I started to
doubt the Father's rejection of the notion of the Bible alone as a
sole rule of faith. However, a more thorough readthrough
helped to deepen my understanding. Outside of these short
and selected excerpts, I found the Church Fathers regularly
appealing to the tradition of the Apostles, and the necessity of
the Church to interpret the Scriptures. I concluded that if these
Church Fathers had truly adopted sola scriptura, then I
wouldn't be able to find an appeal to any other form of the
Word of God (such as tradition or apostolic authority),
otherwise, they wouldn't be going by the Bible alone.

What I found interesting is that these same Church Fathers,
while upholding the authority of Scripture, also appealed to

---

[14] Tertullian of Carthage, *Against Praxeas*, 11, A.D. 160–235

[15] Hippolytus, Against Heresies, 9, A.D. 235

Sacred Tradition and the Magisterium. Any Church Father that appealed to something other than Scripture, must not have been exclusively practicing sola scriptura. Even Irenaeus as quoted above appealed to what was handed down from the Apostles, especially when Scripture was silent or absent. Perhaps more clearly phrased, when Scripture alone was insufficient to resolve.

Tertullian also shared this view of Sacred Tradition as what the church has handed down:

> " *Since this is the case, in order that the truth may be adjudged to belong to us, "as many as walk according to the rule," which the church has handed down from the Apostles, the Apostles from Christ, and Christ from God, the reason of our position is clear; when it determines that heretics ought not to be allowed to challenge an appeal to the Scriptures, since we, without the Scriptures, prove that they have nothing to do with the Scriptures. For as they are heretics, they cannot be true Christians, because it is not from Christ that they get that which they pursue of their own mere choice, and from the pursuit incur and admit the name of heretics. Thus, not being Christians, they have acquired no right to the Christian Scriptures; and it may be very fairly said to them, "Who are you? When and whence did you come?" (Tertullian).* [16]

Lastly, we address the conflicting words of Hippolytus:

---

[16] Tertullian, Prescription Against the Heretics, 37, A.D. 200

&& Therefore let us not prove ourselves unbelieving, lest the word spoken be fulfilled in us. Let us believe then, dear brethren, according to the tradition of the apostles, that God the Word came down from heaven, (and entered) into the holy Virgin Mary" (Hippolytus). [17]

As it seems, Hippolytus, among the other Fathers, adhered also to the Sacred Tradition. The more I searched the early Church writings the more this became apparent.

One final important distinction in the writings of the Church Fathers is the contrast between the formal and material sufficiency of Scripture. Material sufficiency of Scripture recognizes that all Christian doctrine is found in some form (either fully or in seed form) in the Sacred Writings. The Catholic Church has always held to this, and this is what the Church Fathers echo for us across the ages. Formal sufficiency of Scripture suggests that everything believed by Christians is found only in the written Scriptures (this is the position of the Reformers who proposed sola scriptura). Since essential beliefs such as the Canon (among the others I listed) are not found entirely in Scripture alone, this ideology didn't hold weight in my discerning of this practice.

There is excerpt after excerpt from the Church Fathers speaking (at least to a degree) of the sufficiency of Scripture. The overwhelming majority, are speaking about material sufficiency. For any anomalies, we also remember that not all of the Church Fathers agreed on all matters, and not all the Church Fathers wrote inerrantly. Their writings are not

---

[17] Hippolytus, Against Heresies, 9, A.D. 235

Scripture. However, the common thread (by a long shot) is that the Word of God is transmitted both through the Sacred Scriptures as well as Sacred Tradition, handed down from the Apostles, and upheld by the Church, the "pillar and foundation of the truth" (1 Timothy 3:15).

After all of these many hours of discussion, examination of Scripture passages, and testimony from the Church Fathers, the answer seemed simple and clear. Before there was a finished Bible, the Word of God existed inside a living Church. I realized it was not a solo performance. God was allowing it to work together like harmonies. The Word of God in the forms of Sacred Scripture and Sacred Tradition were handed down and given to the Church, to be upheld by the Magisterium. They were all working together, pointing towards the magnificence of God. So how could it seem rational that this form of the Word of God be dismissed 1500 years later (at the Reformation)?

8

THE CANON OF SCRIPTURE

A great stumbling block along the way in the various discussions I had with non-Catholic Christians, is the issue of Canon. The Catholic Church holds to the seventy-three books of Sacred Scripture. Protestant communities hold there are only sixty-six. Both agree on the New Testament Canon of twenty-seven books, leaving the disagreement surrounding the contents of the Old Testament. This seemed slightly odd to me. As far as Christians are concerned, we have the testimony of when our Messiah has come, so why does the account of the Old Testament bear so much weight? Nonetheless, I began to investigate why this was such an issue.

Usually, this discussion was brought about with a Protestant claim that the Catholic Church "added" books to the Bible at the Council of Trent in the Sixteenth Century. For most of my life up until this point, because I didn't know any different, I believed this to be the case. Trent did proclaim dogmatically the books of the Old Testament, paired with the New Testament totalling seventy-three, and even listed them.

What I didn't realize is the reason why. What many Christians (myself included) fail to remember is that councils are almost exclusively called to resolve a heresy or issue that has arisen in the church. So I looked at what issues might have led up to the Council of Trent, and sure enough, this council was in response to the greatest divorce and cause of division in history, the Protestant Reformation.

The Reformers at that time were calling for change within the church in two forms. First, in the way of corruption. Certain individual clergy were abusing power for personal gain. Even today, as Catholics we agree, that personal reform was needed then, and it is needed now, not just among the clergy, but in the life of every single Christian. However, the second type of reform they were calling for was theological. The five solas were proclaimed by the Reformers, and under each category included other long-held doctrines which they therefore began to reject (such as Purgatory, penance, loss of salvation, the relationship between faith and works, etc.). One in particular was the Canon of Scripture.

Martin Luther's foremost appeal was that we are saved by "faith alone". In his translation of Scripture in Romans 3:28, he actually went on to add the word "alone" following, "For we maintain that a person is justified by faith". It was in light of this discovery, that a motivation to remove certain books became apparent.

However, what I didn't realize at first, was that the books he wished to remove, were not only seven from the Old Testament, but also Hebrews, Revelation, and James from the New Testament. One can quickly assume why these particular books were problematic for him. The glaring contraction of Luther's "faith alone" hypothesis, is directly rebutted by the words of Scripture, "You see that a person is justified by works and not by faith alone" (James 2:24 ESV). Hebrews and Revelation also echo the necessity and role of works in regard to salvation. As do many of the books in question from the Old Testament.

Thankfully, Luther eventually added these three New Testament books back into his canon, while still holding personal aversion to their content which seemed contrary to his proposal of "sola fida", or salvation by faith alone.

Circling back to the first assertion, that the Catholic Church added seven books (1 and 2 Maccabees, Tobit, Judith, Sirach, Wisdom and Baruch, as well as additional sections of the Books of Daniel and Esther) to the Bible in the Sixteenth Century, we can start to see the issue with more clarity. As I began to investigate why this council was called in the first place, it became obvious that it was in response to a new heresy, not only of sola fida but also the Canon of Scripture.

So my question remained, did the Catholic Church actually *add* books to the Bible at Trent? It appears as though they did make a dogmatic decree recognizing the firm Canon. What I wondered was if this was a new teaching, or merely defining dogmatically a long-held teaching that had been affirmed across history, in response to the issue those around during the Reformation.

So just like all the other issues that had arisen on my journey in seeking the historical Christian faith, I went to the councils of history.

The Council of Rome in 382 A.D. declared:

❝ *Now indeed we must treat of the divine scriptures, what the universal Catholic Church accepts and what she ought to shun. The order of the Old Testament begins here: Genesis, one book; Exodus, one book; Leviticus, one book;*

Numbers, one book; Deuteronomy, one book; Joshua [Son of] Nave, one book; Judges, one book; Ruth, one book; Kings, four books [that is, 1 and 2 Samuel and 1 and 2 Kings]; Paralipomenon [Chronicles], two books; Psalms, one book; Solomon, three books: Proverbs, one book, Ecclesiastes, one book, [and] Canticle of Canticles [Song of Songs], one book; likewise Wisdom, one book; Ecclesiasticus [Sirach], one book . . . . Likewise the order of the historical [books]: Job, one book; Tobit, one book; Esdras, two books [Ezra and Nehemiah]; Esther, one book; Judith, one book; Maccabees, two books" (The Council of Rome). [18]

The Council of Hippo in 393 A.D. stated:

" *[It has been decided] that besides the canonical scriptures nothing be read in church under the name of divine Scripture. But the canonical scriptures are as follows: Genesis, Exodus, Leviticus, Numbers, Deuteronomy, Joshua the Son of Nun, Judges, Ruth, the Kings, four books, the Chronicles, two books, Job, the Psalter, the five books of Solomon [Proverbs, Ecclesiastes, Song of Songs, Wisdom, and a portion of the Psalms], the twelve books of the prophets, Isaiah, Jeremiah, Daniel, Ezekiel, Tobit, Judith, Esther, Ezra, two books, Maccabees, two books..." (The Council of Hippo).* [19]

The Council of Carthage III in 397 A.D. proclaims:

---

[18] The Council of Rome, Decree of Pope Damasus, A.D. 382

[19] The Council of Hippo, Canon 36, A.D. 393

> **"** *[It has been decided] that nothing except the canonical scriptures should be read in the Church under the name of the divine scriptures. But the canonical scriptures are: Genesis, Exodus, Leviticus, Numbers, Deuteronomy, Joshua, Judges, Ruth, four books of Kings, Paralipomenon, two books, Job, the Psalter of David, five books of Solomon, twelve books of the prophets, Isaiah, Jeremiah, Daniel, Ezekiel, Tobit, Judith, Esther, two books of Esdras, two books of the Maccabees..." (Council of Carthage III).* [20]

The answer was quite clear. There was nothing new being decreed. Trent, in the Sixteenth Century, simply ratified what the church had held as true for centuries, all the way back to the Fourth Century. Since 382 A.D., council after council ratified the same list of canonical books, including the seven books which Protestants refer to as apocrypha, however, Catholics call deuterocanonical.

The assertion that the Council of Trent "added" books was gravely skewed. What I discovered is that it was actually the Reformers who rejected those seven books, and removed them from their collection of Scriptures (Canon), departing from a widely accepted practice for over a millennium.

However, I still wondered on what grounds they decided they could simply remove them. Why *those* books, and for what reasoning (apart from Luther's interpretive clashes)? I reached out to a friend and pastor that I highly respect and trust to see

---

[20] The Council of Carthage III Canon 47, A.D. 397

if he could give me some insight as to the reasoning. I was surprised by the reasonableness of his answer.

The seven "extra" books disagreed upon, all stem from the difference between two ancient collections of Scriptures. The Reformers were advocating that Christianity consider only the Hebrew collection as inspired (which omits the deuterocanonical books). The early church seemed to be holding to the tradition of the Septuagint (the Greek translation of the Bible, containing those seven extra books).

I really wanted to dive in to understand the difference between these collections of Scriptures. What I found is that those are not the only collections that have been used by the people of God! Luther and other Reformers reasoned that the Hebrew collection of Scriptures was what was to be held as inspired. The Reformers believed that the Jews held to only the Hebrew Canon. The problem is knowing which sect of Judaism to follow. The Pharisees (one of the numerous sects of Judaism) indeed held to the thirty-nine books of the Old Testament that the Reformers were advocating. However, the Sadducees (another sect of Judaism) only held to the first five books of the Law, known as the Torah.

What I found interesting is that even to this day, Jews still don't have one definitive closed Canon. My pastor friend alluded to the supposed Council of Jamnia (which he admitted may or may not have even taken place, since there is a lack of historical evidence to confirm it). Even if this council did occur, it would have been over forty years after Christ established Christianity and it was convened by only one sect of Jews (a far cry from a unified ruling). Lastly, it was merely a local council.

Part of his rationale for adopting this ideology, was because God gave the Jews the Oracles (referring to the Word of God), as referenced in Romans 2. Yet at this supposed Council of Jamnia, these same Jews rejected the entire New Testament. As I considered this, I couldn't help but feel it superfluous, to trust a canon to those who reject Christ as the Messiah, and therefore the New Testament writings. The reality is that the Jews never had consensus on the Old Testament Canon (having varieties of accepted collections), and probably aren't the group you'd want to entrust this to, since they don't accept Jesus as the Christ!

My Reformed pastor friend went on to suggest that Jesus and the Apostles rejected the Septuagint (Greek) collection of Scriptures in favour of the Hebrew Canon. He suggested that there are no direct quotes to the deuterocanonicals (those seven extra books) in it, therefore concluding the Hebrew collection is superior. However, upon investigation, what I realized is that similarly missing in the New Testament are quotes from eight other Old Testament books including the Song of Songs (for example). Jesus Himself doesn't quote from all of the Hebrew books. I asked my Reformed friend rhetorically if that would mean we would have to reject those books absent as well. Of course, he agreed with the unreasonableness of that.

Upon further investigation, I found that when the New Testament does quote from the Old Testament, two-thirds of the quotations are from the Septuagint (the collection containing the extra seven books). Jesus, as recorded by the inspired authors quotes from the very collection of Scriptures that is supposed to be rejected. I had to conclude that if Jesus was against the Greek translation, the Septuagint Canon, why would He quote from it majoritively?

My friend interrupted my thought process, suggesting that since Jesus Himself didn't quote any of the deuterocanonical books, therefore, He must not have considered them inspired. So once again, I looked at all of the Old Testament references that Jesus quoted. Missing from that collection were Ruth, Ezra and numerous other Old Testament books. I asked my friend again, did Christ not consider those inspired either?

The reality is that the Scriptures have developed over salvation history. Genesis wasn't even written down for centuries. For many generations, all the Jews had for Scripture was the Law (the Torah), the first five books of the Bible. Eventually along came the prophets. However, several hundred years before Christ came onto the scene, as the common language began to shift from Hebrew to Greek, more inspired writings continued, but not in the Hebrew language. The reason the Hebrew Canon (that the Reformers proposed) was titled that, is because it contained only Old Testament writings written in the Hebrew language.

The Septuagint collection, contained all those writings found in the Hebrew Bible, except they were translated into the common language of Greek. Moreover, in the centuries leading up to Christ, revelation did not cease. Greek authors continued to be faithful in scribing the Word of God, in Greek, and passing it on to future generations.

The Septuagint Canon (containing the seven extra books) was used commonly at the time of Christ. All seven of the deuterocanonical books were written between the period of the Hebrew Bible and Christ's coming (approximately 400 years).

This Greek collection was quoted from the most by New Testament authors and what I realized as I scoured history is that this was the collection of Old Testament books considered inspired for close to a millennium and a half (right up until the Reformation). It was good enough for Jesus, the Apostles, the New Testament authors, sects of Jews, and the people of God for more than a thousand years. I felt secure in accepting it as well.

While the Church Fathers have varying opinions on which books to accept, I could clearly see that this Canon of Scripture was not an invention by the Roman Catholic Church at Trent, but a rich preservation of the Word of God across history.

Since the Council of Rome in 382 A.D., the Church decided upon a Canon of forty-six Old Testament books and twenty-seven in the New Testament. This decision was ratified by the councils at Hippo (393 A.D.), Carthage (397 A.D., 419 A.D.), II Nicea (787 A.D.), Florence (1442 A.D.), and finally dogmatically decreed at Trent (1546 A.D.). This proclamation put to rest any doubt (introduced by the Reformers). Even earlier, Church Fathers such as Jerome, Origen, Cyril of Jerusalem, and Athanasius gave us the seed for a closed Canon, and the Church has ratified and preserved it.

One interesting consideration that came out of this thought process, was who would have the authority to declare which books are inspired in the first place. Scripture gives no criteria. Scripture didn't come with a complete list of books. Should we trust the Jews? But how can we since they reject Jesus as the Messiah and they reject the entire New Testament? Even if we did follow their canon, which one do we go with since they had several? It seems like the only way to know what the Word of God is, is to test it against the historical testimony and tradition of the Church. We would have to inspect which writings are in line with the tradition handed down by the Apostles. All of this kept pointing me in the direction and necessity of a Church instituted by Christ with the authority to decide these matters. Sadly, my observation of both Protestantism and Eastern Orthodoxy was that they are without a mechanism to definitively resolve this very dilemma.

9

HIERARCHY

At the end of the day, with all of the various denominations I witnessed, what I was wrestling with was that no one could tell me definitively what truth is. Everyone was either confident in their understanding of truth, even if their apologetic argument for it was weak, or rather, they considered the subject matter a "grey area". Whenever I raised the question, it was usually met with "You just need to have faith". And it's true, faith is required, but I also wanted definitive answers. Surely Christ gave us His revelation for salvation so that we can know what it is, definitively.

Even the more specific questions I brought up still didn't find resolve. I recall a time when I asked a Reformed friend about John 3:3-5 and its relation to Baptism. Some Reformers appeal to an interpretation of being born of "water" and "spirit" to refer to the water of your mother's womb, and then being saved through faith (alone), not Baptism. Lutherans on the other hand, couple this passage with Titus 3:5-6 to claim that being born of "water and spirit" refers to Baptism's salvific nature. Even among Reformers, there is no clear answer.

There are numerous interpretations of just one passage. It seemed to me like each denomination would string different passages together to accommodate their theology. All of them appeal to Scripture. So who was right? Who had the correct hermeneutic? This is just one simple frustration that kept popping up around every corner.

In my mind and heart, I knew that if Jesus instituted a Church, and entrusted one true deposit of faith to be handed down from the Apostles to future generations, then surely He intended us for us to be able to know the fullness of truth. Surely He didn't say, "This I leave you, now go and do your best to figure it out yourselves…". If He left us merely a book, then we've done a terrible job figuring out what it means with the vast array of denominations today and division in the church. Some would suggest that He gave us the Holy Spirit as a helper and guide. This is true, but if that is solely what individuals are to rely on then the Holy Spirit has done a terrible job. Surely that can't be the case. Perhaps more obviously, *we* are the problem, not the Holy Spirit.

As I have already covered in my search for the historic Christianity of the early church, I unearthed the mechanism they used to resolve heresies, which were councils (starting in Acts 15 and continuing on through the ages). However, what I desired was a better understanding of if there was a hierarchy and authority structure in the Church. Some denominations have pastors, some elders, and some overseers. The Eastern Orthodox and the Roman Catholic Church have deacons, priests, and bishops. What was missing for me was the visible structure, found at least in some form in the early Biblical Church, leading up to today.

I'm pretty sure just about everyone can look through the Scriptures and recognize that Christ Himself appointed Apostles and gave them a leadership role. What most of my Reformed friends would suggest, however, is that any authority they might have had, died with them. In my mind, that seemed odd. Why would Jesus institute a Church, and hand-pick leaders to bring the Gospel to the ends of the earth, and yet by the end of the lifetime of the Apostles, this commissioning would have failed to come to fruition? Surely, Christ must have intended His Church to function in perpetuity, until all come to the knowledge of God.

It wasn't until I started counting all of the Apostles I found in Scripture that it dawned on me, that of course there were successors. Yes, there were the Twelve, however, after Judas betrayed Jesus, and hanged himself, the first order of business for the Church was to "Let another take his office" (Acts 1:20 ESV). The Greek word used for office is "episkopos" which translates to "bishoprics". Matthias is appointed to fill Judas' office (or bishopric) of Apostleship, and so on. As I turned to the New Testament I started to notice that not just the original Twelve were appointed, but numerous others as well including:

* James, head of the Jerusalem church (Galatians 1:19).
* Barnabas (Acts 14:14).
* Paul (Acts 14:14).
* Apollos (Corinthians 4:6-9).
* Timothy and Silvanus (1 Thessalonians 1:1, 2:6).
* Epaphroditus (Philippians 2:25).
* Two unnamed Apostles (2 Corinthians 8:23).

So who were these men? They are called Apostles as well. They had a leadership role in the Church. They held an office of "episkopos" (in Greek) or what is translated as "bishop". But who gave them that authority? Scripture once again became clear, that there was always an intent to continue this hierarchy in the Church, beyond the original Twelve:

> *" This is why I left you in Crete, so that you might put what remained into order, and appoint elders in every town as I directed you" (Titus 1:5).*

> *" And the things you have heard me say in the presence of many witnesses entrust to reliable people who will also be qualified to teach others" (2 Timothy 2:2).*

Paul ordained Timothy who was instructed to ordain others as well. This was not just in the beginning, but until everyone comes to attain the knowledge of God:

> *" He gave the Apostles, the prophets, the evangelists, the shepherds and teachers, to equip the saints for the work of ministry, for building up the body of Christ, until we all attain to the unity of the faith and of the knowledge of the Son of God" (Ephesians 4:11-13).*

What became quite apparent to me is that Christ's institution of the Apostles was always considered to be a continuation of succession (one Apostle ordains another, and then another, and another)... This was demonstrated vividly in the New Testament, and explains why, what started with twelve Apostles, kept multiplying.

Unsure of how to answer this dilemma from a Reformed perspective, I reflected back on the councils. In Acts 15 it was the Apostles, their successors and presbyters who proclaimed the decree (binding on all Christians). In 1 John 4:6, we are reminded:

> *" We [the Apostles] are from God, and whoever knows God listens to us; but whoever is not from God does not listen to us. This is how we recognize the Spirit of truth and the spirit of falsehood" (1 John 4:6).*

How do we know truth? We listen to the Apostles (and their successors). If we don't, we are not of God. This is how we distinguish between truth and falsehood. We must listen to the Apostles. Council after council across history, starting with Jerusalem (Acts 15), has demonstrated this hierarchy and structure. Successors of the Apostles have, through the guidance of the Holy Spirit, given us the Canon of Scripture, the articulation of the Trinity, the Hypostatic Union, and many other important tenets of the faith.

The common thread, however, to be able to test falsehood against truth, was proving apostolic succession. Even the Apostle Paul (who was not one of the original Twelve, but came after them) goes to lengths to explain and prove his authority and the origin of his apostolic office at the beginning of the book of Galatians. Why would he do this, if not to ensure his listeners trusted the source of his message as authentic? This is how the fullness of truth is validated. Truth is transferred down from the Apostles, in an unbroken line of succession.

As I looked at the early Church, I could see the continuity of this apostolic authority and succession. The Church Fathers themselves would document the line of succession. Today, the

Eastern Orthodox Church and Roman Catholic Church can trace their modern-day bishops in an unbroken chain back to the beginning. This is an amazing mechanism of the church as a way to protect the faith Christ entrusted to her, "the gates of Hades will not overcome it" (Matthew 16:18). This means there will never be a time in history when His Church will fall into apostasy. There will always be a direct connection to the fullness of truth. It will never be cut off, even though some might deflect from it.

When I began to explore this avenue of apostolic succession, one of the main arguments given to me by Reformed friends against it was "sola ecclesia". This criticism, of rejecting sola scriptura and recognizing apostolic authority and succession, suggests that the Church is somehow the final authority and fully sufficient. Yet, the Church is positioned to be the "pillar and foundation of truth" (1 Timothy 3:15). It supports and upholds the Word of God, passed down from the Apostles, through the apostolic line.

I could see how efficacious apostolic authority and succession were across history. I could see the authority of the councils in action right from the beginning. However, what didn't seem to fit into place yet, was the Papacy.

10

THE PAPACY

The teaching of the Papacy is probably one of the most hated, scrutinized and misunderstood. I could observe this papal dilemma even from my own experience. By this point in my journey, I was pretty much on board with Eastern Orthodoxy. What seemed much more difficult to grasp, let alone articulate, was how one guy could hold all the authority.

In the context of a council, I could get behind it. When the Holy Spirit leads and guides the council, it seems more democratic. However, comparing the role of the Pope to the vile dictators across history seemed like it would be opening a door to disaster.

Surely if there was one guy in charge, he could make extreme and wild changes to doctrine. He could, through his own interpretations and preferences, change the entire course that is the Church. I pictured it like a captain steering a vessel across the ocean. If the wrong captain is put in charge, the destination can change quite quickly (whether through malice or inadequacy for the job).

I definitely sympathize with those who struggle to grasp how the Papacy could be God-willed. Surely, it would open up His teachings to distortion and mutilation. We've seen enough worldly dictators demonstrate the flaws of humanity that surely God wouldn't build His Church in such a fashion.

I honestly didn't know where to start. So before I even tackled what the early Church Fathers held or even what Scripture said, I examined the Papacy across history. What I was really looking for was an example of a Pope who departed from the tradition handed down by the Apostles and proclaimed it binding on the faithful. In my mind, the easiest way to prove the role of the Pope as null and void was to simply demonstrate (at least) one example of a man who departed from orthodox teaching.

If I could simply find even just one Pope that changed a long-held dogma, it would contradict the one true Church. So I started to dig. I found many Popes who were less than virtuous. The first of the lowlight reel included Pope Alexander VI in the Fifteenth Century, who bought the Papacy and bribed his fellow electors. He appointed his friends and relatives into positions of power and killed off the Cardinals who dissented from him. He also fathered several children with his numerous mistresses.

Another exceptional example was Pope Stephen VI, who in the Ninth Century had his predecessor and arch-rival exhumed (though having been dead for some time), and then fully dressed in Papal robes to stand trial. His body was then dragged through the streets and dumped into the Tiber River. He sounded like a really classy gentleman.

As I discovered example after example of men with less than heroic character and virtue, what I didn't find was a change in any binding dogma of the faith. Some of these men did despicable things. Yet, despite their lack of virtue, didn't change the deposit of faith handed down from the Apostles.

Some might suggest that through their sinful actions or inaction, they disqualified Catholicism from the one true church. In fact, this was the leading charge brought up to me against the Catholic Church. How can it be the one true faith, if her leaders across the ages have been vile and corrupt? Many people mentioned these awful leaders, and how individuals killed one another in the name of religion.

As I reflected on this dilemma, I could only be left with the fact that every single religion known to man has possessed those who do not measure up to the ideology and theology they profess. Catholicism doesn't call us to, "do what they do", as even Jesus pointed out in Matthew 23:3, that the leadership of God's people has been given authority. Jesus simply instructs us that we must, "be careful to do everything they tell you" (Matthew 23:3).

Considering this further I was also reminded of the people that Jesus hand-picked to be leaders and given authority. Peter denied Jesus (Luke 22:54-62). Peter stood "condemned" (Galatians 2:11) for not acting in accordance with what he was teaching. Judas betrayed Jesus (Luke 22:4-6). All of the Apostles except John abandoned our Messiah. Surely if impeccability was required for the job, Jesus Himself failed in selecting the right crew.

The more I considered the failures of even the Apostles, the more I was reminded that none of us are perfect. We all fail to measure up. We all sin. We all have deficiencies. We have all failed to act, and have acted poorly. However, despite this, God still works through us. Despite the frailty of the successors across the ages, the Holy Spirit has still led, guarded and protected the deposit of faith Christ gave us. Perhaps the impeccability of its followers isn't the determinant of whether a particular religion is true. If it were, no religion would pass that test, disqualifying all of them (including every denomination of Christianity).

A quick glance across history and it's quite evident that doctrine develops. It doesn't outright change, or contradict itself, but the Church's understanding of certain truths has developed over the years. The way certain truths have been communicated and expounded upon has progressed. Perhaps a simplistic example might be one of the Ten Commandments, "Thou shall not kill" (Exodus 20:13 KJV). This command in its most fundamental phrasing doesn't leave much in the way of exceptions. As God continued to lead His chosen people the Israelites, He deepened their understanding of this law, even creating "safe villages" for those fleeing from justice who were "wrongfully" charged or misunderstood (Exodus 21:12-13). As the centuries continued, our understanding of the Law has spawned into the area of conflict inciting "just war". Even finding certain circumstances where it may have been feasible over the ages to incite the death penalty, if for public safety or the common good.

This development took hundreds of years. We see a natural progression, a logical development as the Holy Spirit has led and guided the Church into deeper understanding. The same is true with other teachings as well such as the formulation of the Trinity and Hypostatic Union.

What I found quite fascinating, is that though there are some semantic examples, all of them seemed to be easily understood through the lens of development. Many of them weren't even a doctrine, but rather simply a discipline (such as vestments or celibacy). The Catholic Church has never claimed infallible domain over discipline (or practices).

Papal infallibility is exercised when the Pope intends to teach, by virtue of his supreme authority, on a matter of faith and morals, to the whole Church. The Church teaches that when this criteria is met, this dogmatic proclamation is preserved from error by the Holy Spirit. This doesn't necessarily mean the Pontiff *will* speak, especially when there is a need. It also is limited to matters of faith and morals. So if a Pope declared the moon is made of cheese, not only would that statement be scientifically incorrect, but it also wouldn't be infallible, because it is outside the domain of his authority (not being related to faith and morals).

What's interesting is that in the two thousand years of the history of the Catholic Church, there has never been a dogma that has ever changed. People would be surprised to know just how rarely Papal Infallibility has been enacted by a Pope. Just because Popes have had this power, what we see is that it is seldom exercised, and in most cases has only been done so after consulting other bishops.

More common is the infallibility of the Church, found in the bishops. The Dogmatic Constitution on the Church states:

> " *The infallibility promised to the Church resides also in the body of Bishops when that body exercises the supreme magisterium with the successor of Peter"* (Lumen Gentium). [21]

---

[21] Vatican Council II, *Lumen Gentium*, No. 25.

However, as I traversed this issue, I couldn't help but wonder, if we have councils of bishops (successors of Apostles), who are able to give us infallible dogma, then why do we have or need a Pope? This caused me to lean into Scripture, which is where it all started to connect.

The very first time Jesus met Simon (John 1:42), Jesus gave him a new name, "Peter" or "Cephas" (in Aramaic). The Scriptures pay close attention to preserving that name. What is interesting is that was not a name at the time. In Aramaic, the word Cephas means only one thing, "rock". It would be like Jesus walking up to John and saying, "Your new name is tree". This is the first and most important point of recognition. Jesus renames Simon, to Cephas—"rock".

In Matthew 16:13, Jesus asks His Apostles, "Who do people say the Son of Man is?". Simon Peter having received special inspiration from God proclaims, "You are the Messiah, the Son of the living God" (Matthew 16:16). In the presence of the other Apostles, Jesus says:

> " *Blessed are you Simon… I tell you that you are Peter [which means 'rock'], and on this rock I will build my church" (Matthew 16:18).*

Many are resistant to seeing the connection between those two events. For me, however, when this was pointed out, I couldn't unsee it. Jesus meets Simon, gives him a new name (a name that has never been used as a name), a name which literally means "rock", then takes him (and the other Apostles) on top of a giant rock, and says to *Simon* alone, in the presence of the other Apostles, "You are Peter [rock], and on this rock I will be my church".

Over the course of the numerous conversations I had on this one passage with Reformed pastors, there were a plethora of explanations. The variety of assertions included that Peter's faith is the rock, or that Peter's proclamation of Jesus as the Messiah is the rock. However, the most commonly held interpretation by Reformers, and the most extreme, is that Jesus was actually diminishing Peter, by contrasting him (Simon) with the true rock upon which Christ will build His church.

One of the age-old debates is the interpretation of the Greek words used for rock in Matthew 16:18. One would assume if Peter is the rock that Jesus is talking about in both cases, then the exact same word would be used. On the surface, this argument seemed to make sense. However, what people much smarter than me (someone who barely passed grammar school) point out is that would be grammatically impossible.

The text in Greek reads, "You are 'Petros', and on this 'petra' I will build my church". So, why are these two words, though a variation of the same word for rock, different? If Peter is the rock, wouldn't they be exactly the same? What I learned, which is different from the English language, is that Koine Greek has both masculine and feminine nouns. Peter is a man. Yet the word for rock is a feminine noun ("petra"). It would be grammatically incorrect to use the feminine form of the noun for a man. Therefore, the inspired author did the only thing he could, and changed the form of the feminine "petra", to the masculine "Petros" since Peter is a man. In fact, if he had used "petra" for Peter, it would have been grammatically incorrect.

The other argument, that many of the Reformed pastors who dialogued with me on this issue claimed, was that petros should translate as "little pebble" and petra as "large stone". This would seem to pit Peter against the rock, diminishing Peter (as a small pebble) from the rock of faith (the large stone). When I investigated this interpretation I found that petra and petros can mean large stone and little pebble in Greek. However, not in the dialect of Koine Greek that this was written. In Koine, there is no such distinction. We miss the obvious play on words in Greek.

Perhaps the more apparent question is what did the early church believe about Peter as the rock? How did they understand Jesus' dramatic unfolding of events at Caesarea Philippi?

St. John Chrysostom said regarding Matthew 16, "Upon this rock I will build my church" and continued by stating, "that is, on the faith of his confession". [22] Many of my esteemed Reformed friends would share this quote to support the idea that even the early church didn't believe Peter to be the rock. However, if we continue reading Chrysostom's homilies, he clarifies:

" *[Peter] became a foundation of the Church" (St. John Chrysostom).* [23]

---

[22] Chrysostom, J. (A.D. 386-397) Homily 3 on Matthew. In P. Schaff (Ed.), Nicene and Post-Nicene Fathers, First Series, Vol. 10 (NPNF1 X:19).

[23] Chrysostom, J. (A.D. 386-397) Homily 3 on Matthew. In P. Schaff (Ed.), Nicene and Post-Nicene Fathers, First Series, Vol. 10 (NPNF1 X:19).

" *Peter… the foundation of the faith" (St. John Chrysostom).* [24]

" *Peter, that the head of the Apostles, the first in the Church, the friend of Christ, who received the revelation not from man but from the Father… this Peter, and when I say Peter, I mean the unbroken rock, the unshaken foundation, the great apostle, the first of the disciples, the first called, the first to obey" (St. John Chrysostom).* [25]

One last minor, yet important detail is that while the earliest manuscripts we have recovered are written in Koine Greek, there is historical evidence that points to the fact that the Gospel of Matthew was originally written in Aramaic first, and then translated into Greek. Jesus spoke these words to Peter in Aramaic. There is only one word for "rock" in Aramaic, which is "Cephas". We see this preserved for us in the New Testament (Galatians 2:14 and John 1:42). And there is only one person with the name Cephas—Simon Peter. We can see this demonstrated similarly in other languages as well, such as French, "You are Pierre, and on this Pierre I will build my church". In English, we miss the linguistic play on words, that the New Testament authors so cleverly gave us. When Jesus spoke this in Aramaic he said, "You are Cephas and on this Cephas I will build my church" (Matthew 16:18). Peter is the rock.

---

[24] Chrysostom, J. (A.D. 386-397). Homily on the Ten Thousand Talents (Hom. de decem mille talentis), Chapman 74

[25] Chrysostom, J. (A.D. 386-397). *Almsgiving 3:4*, Chapman 74

However, I came to eventually realize, whether or not our interpretation of Peter being the rock is correct or not, it doesn't actually matter as much as we like to think. It seemed clear to me as I wrestled with this passage on Peter's authority and role, that what happened immediately after is much more telling.

After Jesus promises to build His Church, He turns to Peter and says:

" *I will give you the keys of the kingdom of heaven; whatever you bind on earth will be bound in heaven, and whatever you loose on earth will be loosed in heaven"* *(Matthew 16:19).*

In Greek the tense of the word, "you" (indicating who Jesus is talking to) is singular. He's not speaking to all the Apostles, just Peter alone. Peter alone is given the keys of the Kingdom of Heaven. No other Apostle was given this special appointment to bear the keys.

This brings up a whole new connection and continuation of God's Kingdom. After months of squabbling over whose interpretation regarding "this rock" was correct, it was pointed out to me that it's actually the keys that give this passage a deeper meaning and striking impact. The inspired author seems to be harkening back to an Old Testament text and prophecy from Isaiah 22:20-23. In God's Kingdom of the Old Testament, there was a King. This Kingdom of David also had a chief steward (or "prime" minister). This royal steward was second in command. They were given authority by the King to rule the Kingdom, holding the keys of the Kingdom:

" *In that day I will summon my servant, Eliakim son of Hilkiah. I will clothe him with your robe and fasten your sash around him and hand your authority over to him. He will be a father to those who live in Jerusalem and to the people of Judah. I will place on his shoulder the key to the house of David; what he opens no one can shut, and what he shuts no one can open. I will drive him like a peg into a firm place; he will become a seat of honor for the house of his father"* (Isaiah 22:20-23).

This new steward that is to come will not only bear the Keys of the Kingdom of the house of David (the Kingdom of Jesus). He will also be a "father" to the people, robed with the King's "authority", a "seat" of honour, a "peg" of firm foundation. Jesus quotes this passage almost verbatim.

The book of Revelation also reaffirms these keys, "These are the words of him who is holy and true, who holds the key of David. What he opens no one can shut, and what he shuts no one can open" (Revelation 3:7).

As I looked at this old Kingdom the parallels were apparent. Jesus, the rightful heir to the throne of the Kingdom of David, delegates His authority to Peter, the rock on which He built His Church, and gives him the Keys. Peter was the first to hold the office of chief steward under the Kingship of Christ. Continuing in the succession of the Kingdom of David, this office has successors with authority to shepherd the Kingdom.

Looking back through the Scriptures after this, it became plain to point out Peter's role. Peter seemed to exercise a more supreme authority over the Apostles. In Acts 1, Peter presides over the group to elect the successor to Judas' office of Apostleship. Peter chaired a special authority over the first council of Jerusalem (Acts 15), having given his instruction, the audience of Apostles and elders fell quiet. Afterwards, James affirmed what Peter stated. It's also Peter who preached at Pentecost, leading among the other Apostles. When the names of the Apostles are listed, Peter's name is almost always listed first. [26] Judas' name is almost always listed last. That is not a coincidence. Many other times it's, "Peter, and the rest of the Apostles". [27] In John 21:17, Peter alone was singled out and made shepherd, instructed by Jesus to "feed my sheep". Peter was called "chief" or "first" among the Apostles (Matthew 10:2), even though it was Andrew whom Jesus met and called first (John 1:40-42). Jesus prays for Peter specifically, "That your faith may not fail. And when you have turned back, strengthen your brothers" (Luke 22:32). Sometimes we miss these subtle clues through the lens of our current culture and two-millennium of separation. The early Church Fathers echo this primacy given to Peter, passed down through succession:

❝ *Was anything withheld from the knowledge of Peter, who is called 'the rock on which the Church would be built' [Matthew 16:18] with the power of 'loosing and binding in Heaven and on earth?"* (Tertullian). [28]

---

26 Matthew 10:1-4, Mark 3:16-19, Luke 6:14-16, Acts 1:13

27 Luke 9:32, Acts 2:37

28 Tertullian, Demurrer Against the Heretics, 22, A.D. 200

❝ Look at [Peter], the great foundation of the Church, that most solid of rocks, upon whom Christ built the Church" (Origen). [29]

❝ You cannot deny that you do know that upon Peter first in the city of Rome was bestowed the episcopal cathedra, on which sat Peter, the head of the Apostles (for which reason he was called Cephas), that, in this one cathedra, unity should be preserved by all" (Optatus). [30]

Apart from these select quotes, there are a plethora of Church Fathers acknowledging Peter as the rock and his primacy. This is simply how the universal church at large interpreted and understood what Jesus said in Matthew 16:18-19. What one should also take note of is the lack of controversy documented throughout history. We clearly see Peter's primacy referenced, acknowledged and exercised, and yet we see almost no objection, until the Eastern Orthodox schism almost 1000 years later.

There are far too many quotes regarding Peter's primacy and special role, from the early Church Fathers to be able to share here. I'd invite you to go read them for yourself, as they paint a clear picture of how even in the first few centuries, the Church recognized the special role of the bishop of Rome as shepherd of the universal Church, holding the Keys of the Kingdom.

---

[29] Origen, Homilies on Exodus, 5:4, A.D. 248

[30] Optatus, Schism of the Donatists, 2:2, A.D. 367

One historical example I found quite compelling is near the end of the First Century. Issues arose in the church in Corinth. Does that sound familiar? The Apostle John, one of the original Apostles was still alive and living in Ephesus (across the Aegean Sea). However, instead of the Corinthians appealing to a living Apostle (who was much closer), they wrote all the way to Clement, the bishop of Rome (and third Pope), as documented by Second Century bishop Irenaeus of Lyons. [31] Clement of Rome wrote a rather authoritative and direct letter admonishing them. It made me wonder why. Why would they travel such a great distance to Rome, to appeal to a successor of a successor of an Apostle (outside of his geographical jurisdiction), when they had one of the originals just across the pond?

This example indicated to me that they quite clearly understood that the bishop of Rome had the authority to resolve disputes in the Church. It seemed like the early Church had a hierarchical structure in place from the beginning.

Over and over again as I would go down the path of this discussion with my Reformed counterparts, the fundamental obstacle was a person having to surrender to the authority of hierarchy. I remember after hours of exhaustive discussion, someone asking me frankly, "How can you just listen to some guy in Rome?". Essentially they were honestly asking why they should consider putting their trust in a man, rather than God alone. On the surface, I could see their point.

This was a type of question that tends to get people stirred up. But for me, it gave clarity. As I saw it, non-Catholic

---

[31] St. Irenaeus of Lyons, *Against Heresies*, Book III, Chapter 3 (A.D. 175)

Christians, who claimed to reject the Pope, were making their own little popes. Whether it be a pastor they trust, or their own interpretation or understanding, they were surrendering to the "pope" they gave authority to, all seemingly under the guise of rejecting the corruption of the Papacy. By rejecting the "man" of the Papacy, they were instead just shifting their trust to the "man" of their own interpretation, or trusting the "man" of the pastor they follow.

Unfortunately, with the thousands of denominations and divisions within the church, I didn't see each person's mini-pope as a viable solution. In fact, it seemed more and more obvious that this was the very problem.

11

THE NEW COVENANT

Being on a quest to find the true faith of Christianity, and having witnessed a living, hierarchical Church across the ages, the next question that followed was pondering how one might become part of this Church. What is the normative means of initiation into this family of faith?

Many of my Reformed friends consider the immersion into Christ's covenant to be the moment of their assent of will (or rather, the moment they profess to believe in their mind and heart). What most Christians would agree on, is that there is a difference in status prior to the moment of initiation, versus after. The question is really, what exactly is that initiation process?

In one sense, salvation through the New Covenant could be likened to hopping aboard a great ship (much like Noah's Ark), ready to weather the storm of death and destruction. To stay on land during the great flood would mean death, yet God created a way for His beloved to be saved. Noah and his family were saved by their faith in God, through the ark, by following God. The moment of their initiation was when through faith, they trusted God, listened, and boarded the Ark which had the power to save.

But what if they were tired of waiting for the waters to subside? What if they got tired of the smell of the animals in close proximity? What if they wanted to make a vessel of their own to find land themselves? Surely all of these would be met with their own demise. The only way to remain steadfast in God's promise was to remain in the Ark and continually be renewed in God's covenant.

" *...to those who were disobedient long ago when God waited patiently in the days of Noah while the ark was being built. In it only a few people, eight in all, were saved through water, and this water symbolizes baptism that now saves you also—not the removal of dirt from the body but the pledge of a clear conscience toward God" (1 Peter 3:20-21).*

As Noah's family was saved through the waters of the flood, in the Old Covenant, Peter is saying we are now saved through the waters of Baptism in the New Covenant.

I wanted to understand this New Covenant we as Christians are a part of. I wanted to go back to the Last Supper and try to comprehend what a New Covenant would be, in the context of Jesus, a Jew who kept the Law perfectly, and established a Covenant with us at the Passover, while fulfilling the Old.

There aren't two Gods, one of the Old Testament and one of the New. The same God has established covenants with His people over the centuries of salvation history. If this is true, then I couldn't help but consider that there must be some connection between these Covenants.

Jesus Himself points out this reality in Matthew 5:17, "Do not think that I have come to abolish the Law or the Prophets; I have not come to abolish them but to fulfill them". And in the context of this, I sought to understand this "new" Covenant through the lens of the "old".

Leading up to the time of Christ, if through faith, you desired to be part of the one true faith and to follow God, there was only one way. Circumcision was how the father of a household would commit his family to the Covenant of God. This was how the entire family was saved and brought into the Covenant. Circumcision was the gateway and initiation.

Without it, one could not participate in the sacred rituals, in the Passover, and in the worship. Coming into communion with God was first and foremost obtained by way of this saving act. When I gave this some real consideration, I was thankful to be a Catholic and not a Jew! This is a costly sacrifice. This involves bloodshed and pain. However, without sacrifice, there can be no true Covenant. Simply put, leading up to the time of Christ, if a man were convinced that Judaism was the one true faith instituted by God, they wouldn't truly be under His Covenant by simply an assent of the will. It wasn't enough to believe in their heart and mind. A man would need to undergo the initiation process—circumcision (Exodus 12:48).

This act is not merely symbolic. It wasn't merely just an "outward sign of faith" (what many of my Reformed friends suggest about Baptism), but the act itself brought about what it symbolizes. Through circumcision, one is made part of the family of God and brought into His covenant.

God commanded Abraham:

" *As for you, you must keep my covenant, you and your descendants after you for the generations to come. This is my covenant with you and your descendants after you, the covenant you are to keep: Every male among you shall be circumcised. You are to undergo circumcision, and it will be the sign of the covenant between me and you. For the generations to come every male among you who is eight days old must be circumcised, including those born in your household or bought with money from a foreigner—those who are not your offspring. Whether born in your household or bought with your money, they must be circumcised. My covenant in your flesh is to be an everlasting covenant. Any uncircumcised male, who has not been circumcised in the flesh, will be cut off from his people; he has broken my covenant" (Genesis 17:9-14).*

Abraham and his entire household were brought into the Covenant and family of God through the act of circumcision. This is how they were initiated into God's Covenant. Furthermore, anyone who was not circumcised was "cut off" from God.

Something that struck me as I reflected on this salvific act, was that even babies could be made part of God's family and part of God's Covenant. God instructed them to circumcise on the eighth day. One might ask how a baby can exercise their own faith or choose to be part of God's Covenant. They can't, yet God's salvation is for everyone, including children. The faith of the father brings salvation to the entire household of faith through this sacrifice of obedience.

Jesus, who kept the Law perfectly was also circumcised on the eighth day, "On the eighth day, when it was time to circumcise the child, he was named Jesus, the name the angel had given him before he was conceived" (Luke 2:21).

Abraham wasn't saved by faith *alone*. His family wasn't blessed and brought into the saving Covenant of God by faith alone. However, it was through the act of obedience, through faith in God. Not in his works alone, but obedience through faith. What I came to realize many years later is that wrapped up in the verb (action word), "believe" is this notion of obedience in an ongoing and continual sense.

As I discovered this significance, I began to reflect on what this might mean for the "New Covenant". In Luke 22:20 Jesus said, "This cup is the new covenant in my blood, which is poured out for you". He is instituting a New Covenant, with a new fatherhood of faith, with a new sign of initiation and adoption. So what might this new sign be?

> " *In him you were also circumcised with a circumcision not performed by human hands. Your whole self ruled by the flesh was put off when you were circumcised by Christ, having been buried with him in baptism, in which you were also raised with him through your faith in the working of God, who raised him from the dead. When you were dead in your sins and in the uncircumcision of your flesh, God made you alive with Christ. He forgave us all our sins"* (Colossians 2:11–13).

If you were not circumcised, you were not able to partake in the Old Covenant liturgies such as the Exodus Passover. If you were not circumcised and part of God's family, you were not spared, not saved from the final plague on Egypt and not part of the Exodus. However, this epistle to the Colossians isn't talking about circumcision of the flesh, but rather through

Baptism. It is through Baptism that we are "buried with him" and raised to life through faith.

It became apparent to me that the sign of the New Covenant is Baptism. This is the gateway. This is how one is brought into the family of faith. This is how we are initiated into the covenant of God. When I looked back on that infamous passage of the first council of Jerusalem in Acts 15, this was all so clear. They were arguing about how one is to be made part of the Covenant of God suggesting that, "Unless you are circumcised, according to the custom taught by Moses, you cannot be saved" (Acts 15:1). For centuries circumcision was the gateway into God's Covenant. We can begin to understand why this dilemma arose in the first place. However, we are now in a *New* Covenant, with a new sign: Baptism. That dogmatic degree from Acts 15:28 echos to this day, "It seemed good to the Holy Spirit and to us not to burden you with anything beyond the following requirements…". No, circumcision is no longer required, because Gentiles are welcomed to be part of the New Covenant, to be born anew into the household of God.

Jesus Himself addressed being born again, becoming a new creation specifically. How is it that we are born again? Jesus tells us simply:

> **❝** *Very truly I tell you, no one can see the kingdom of God unless they are born again" (John 3:3).*

Nicodemus was confused by this and asked, "'How can someone be born when they are old?' Nicodemus asked. 'Surely they cannot enter a second time into their mother's womb to be born!'" (John 3:4).

Jesus clarifies:

> 66 *Very truly I tell you, no one can enter the kingdom of God unless they are born of water and the Spirit" (John 3:5).*

As I continued to investigate, I appealed to Scripture to find out how we are born of the Spirit. Numerous passages became plainly clear. It is through water Baptism. Jesus gave the example for us Himself, He went into the water, the Heavens opened up, and the Holy Spirit manifested Himself in the form of a dove and remained on Him (Matthew 3:13-17). We see the sign of Baptism being the water and the effect being the Spirit. Jesus reaffirms this in John 3:5, we must be born of "water and the Spirit".

When we look back at Genesis, we see the parallel between Baptism and creation.

"Now the earth was formless and empty, darkness was over the surface of the deep, and the Spirit of God was hovering over the waters. And God said, 'Let there be light,' and there was light…" (Genesis 1:2-3).

We see that the Earth was dark and empty, similar to our state before being made new. Then the Holy Spirit hovered over the water and God made a new creation. This is what happens in Baptism. God uses water and the Spirit to make a new creation in us. We see a clever divine continuity throughout the Scriptures.

Some of my Reformed friends would argue that there is no correlation between being born again and Baptism. However, right before Jesus stated that we must be born again, He

Himself was baptized. After He stated that we must be born again, Jesus and His disciples went throughout the land baptizing (John 3:22). Jesus' last instruction to His Apostles was specific:

> " *All authority in heaven and on earth has been given to me. Therefore go and make disciples of all nations, baptizing them in the name of the Father and of the Son and of the Holy Spirit, and teaching them to obey everything I have commanded you" (Matthew 28:18-20).*

How were they to "make disciples"? By, "baptizing them" and "teaching them to obey everything I have commanded you" (Matthew 28:19). We become a follower of Christ by believing, being baptized and obeying Christ's commands. This is where our journey begins in the New Covenant.

This reality was evident from the beginning of the church:

> " *When the people heard this, they were cut to the heart and said to Peter and the other Apostles, 'Brothers, what shall we do?' Peter replied, 'Repent and be baptized, every one of you, in the name of Jesus Christ for the forgiveness of your sins. And you will receive the gift of the Holy Spirit. The promise is for you and your children and for all who are far off —for all whom the Lord our God will call'" (Acts 2:37-39).*

" For all of you who were baptized into Christ have clothed yourselves with Christ" (Galatians 3:27).

" Let us draw near to God with a sincere heart and with the full assurance that faith brings, having our hearts sprinkled to cleanse us from a guilty conscience and having our bodies washed with pure water" (Hebrews 10:22).

" I will sprinkle clean water on you, and you will be clean; I will cleanse you from all your impurities and from all your idols. I will give you a new heart and put a new spirit in you; I will remove from you your heart of stone and give you a heart of flesh. And I will put my Spirit in you and move you to follow my decrees and be careful to keep my laws. Then you will live in the land I gave your ancestors; you will be my people, and I will be your God. I will save you from all your uncleanness" (Ezekiel 36:25-29).

Jesus describes to His disciples that they will be "baptized with the Holy Spirit" (Acts 1:4-5), yet when the Holy Spirit is given in numerous instances in the book of Acts, it was "poured out" (Acts 2:17-18, 33).

One of the most obvious and overlooked passages on this matter is from 1 Peter 3. When I came across it for the first time, I couldn't understand how this issue was still up for debate:

" Baptism.. now saves you... not the removal of dirt from the body but the pledge of a clear conscience toward

God. It saves you by the resurrection of Jesus Christ" (1 Peter 3:21).

What I found so fascinating, is that many of my Reformed friends and pastors would argue diligently that "baptism doesn't save you", all the while Scripture literally says the opposite. It's not just a bath. It's not just an "outward profession of faith", rather, it is truly efficacious.

Not only from a Biblical perspective, but the first Christians testify to their understanding of baptismal regeneration. The Didache is one of the most ancient early writings (written around 70 A.D., before the last book of the New Testament was even written). The instruction from the Apostles tells the first Christians:

> " *Concerning baptism, baptize in this manner: Having said all these things beforehand, baptize in the name of the Father and of the Son and of the Holy Spirit in living water [running water or a river]. If there is no living water, baptize in other water; and, if you are not able to use cold water, use warm. If you have neither, pour water three times upon the head in the name of the Father, Son, and Holy Spirit" (Didache).* [32]

In addition to the Didache, I discovered a plethora of Church Fathers, spanning as early as the First Century who reaffirmed that "baptism... now saves", and the understanding that was handed down from Jesus and the Apostles.

---

[32] *Didache*, A.D. 70

> **❝** 'I have heard, sir,' said I [to the Shepherd], 'from some teacher, that there is no other repentance except that which took place when we went down into the water and obtained the remission of our former sins.' He said to me, 'You have heard rightly, for so it is" (Shepherd of Hermans).
> 33

> **❝** As many as are persuaded and believe that what we [Christians] teach and say is true, and undertake to be able to live accordingly . . . are brought by us where there is water, and are regenerated in the same manner in which we were ourselves regenerated. For, in the name of God, the Father and Lord of the universe, and of our Savior Jesus Christ, and of the Holy Spirit, they then receive the washing with water. For Christ also said, 'Except you be born again, you shall not enter into the kingdom of heaven' [John 3:3]" (St. Justin Martyr). 34

This is why the Church from the beginning has always allowed infants to be baptized, through the faith of their parents.

Baptism is the act which enables one to be made part of the Covenant of God. This sign of the New Covenant is, "for you and your children and for all who are far off" (Acts 2:39). Baptism is the *new* circumcision, made without hands, that brings us into the Covenant of God.

---

33 The Shepherd 4:3:1–2 (A.D. 80)

34 St. Justin Martyr, First Apology 61 (A.D. 151)

As I reflected on this continuity of covenants, I began to ponder what this might mean for someone who believes in Christ but wasn't ever baptized. Perhaps they were formed in a faith community that didn't understand the nature of Baptism. I can see how they might be put off by hearing this. Perhaps they even might be made to feel secondary. This right here is a crucial moment in apologetics. This is where many would triumphantly condemn such a person. However, like our patient Heavenly Father, let us journey with someone through this process of understanding with charity rather than abruptly chastising them. This doesn't mean withholding truth, but communicating it through love so that it is received most effectively. In my travels, I've come across many denominations that either don't understand the importance of Baptism or who haven't emphasized it as part of a Christian's faith journey. After all, while the Catholic Church teaches that Baptism is necessary for salvation, it also affirms that God is not bound to the Sacraments. The thief of the cross is a profound example of God working extraordinarily by His grace. What is important to remember is that examples like this are exceptions, not the norm.

We must recognize that we are all in need of continual reformation. When we look to Scripture, there are parts that call us to be transformed and reproved. A personal example of this, which cuts me straight to the heart is from Mark 12:41-44 where a widow placed two small coins into the offering. Jesus says that she gave more than all of the others, "They all gave out of their wealth; but she, out of her poverty, put in everything—all she had to live on" (Mark 12:44). That passage gets me every time. It reminds me that I need to strive to have the love and generosity of that poor widow, not merely giving out of my abundance, but also giving when it hurts and truly costs me.

Perhaps generosity isn't your call to reform. Maybe it's forgiving a brother who has wronged you (Matthew 6:15), or being grateful in all circumstances (1 Thessalonians 5:16-18), or maybe it is understanding the commandments of God, such as Baptism (Mark 16:16). Regardless, we all are on a journey towards the fullness of truth.

Lastly, I will leave this chapter with one of the most controversial statements ever delivered by the Catholic Church (and probably the most misquoted and misunderstood).

" *Outside the Church there is no salvation" (CCC).* [35]

This statement tends to bring an emotional reaction, understandably. How could someone say that one cannot be saved apart from the Church? Yet, often I'm reminded that Christ himself made this bold claim:

" *I am the way and the truth and the life. No one comes to the Father except through me" (John 14:6).*

No one is saved apart from Christ. This is equally offensive. Thankfully, the Catholic Church expounds on what she means by this in the Catechism of the Catholic Church:

---

[35] Catechism of the Catholic Church, Paragraphs 845-846

" *How are we to understand this affirmation, often repeated by the Church Fathers? Re-formulated positively, it means that all salvation comes from Christ the Head through the Church which is his Body: 'Basing itself on Scripture and Tradition, the Council teaches that the Church, a pilgrim now on earth, is necessary for salvation: the one Christ is the mediator and the way of salvation; he is present to us in his body which is the Church. He himself explicitly asserted the necessity of faith and Baptism, and thereby affirmed at the same time the necessity of the Church which men enter through Baptism as through a door. Hence they could not be saved who, knowing that the Catholic Church was founded as necessary by God through Christ, would refuse either to enter it or to remain in it'. This affirmation is not aimed at those who, through no fault of their own, do not know Christ and his Church: 'Those who, through no fault of their own, do not know the Gospel of Christ or his Church, but who nevertheless seek God with a sincere heart, and, moved by grace, try in their actions to do his will as they know it through the dictates of their conscience - those too may achieve eternal salvation'. Although in ways known to himself God can lead those who, through no fault of their own, are ignorant of the Gospel, to that faith without which it is impossible to please him, the Church still has the obligation and also the sacred right to evangelize all men" (CCC).* [36]*

---

[36] [36] Catechism of the Catholic Church, Paragraphs 846-848

Those through no fault of their own, who do not know Christ or His Church, yet by grace are striving to live according to their conscience, the possibility of salvation exists. Let us praise God for His patience in this. I, myself, do not fully understand and comprehend all of the truths of the faith perfectly. Yet, I aim to have a heart that is striving to be continually transformed into the image of God. Our faith in God should stir us to be more conformed to Him and to follow His commands more vigilantly. Likewise, coming to the knowledge of God's commands should foster a more fervent faith in Him.

12

THE NEW PASSOVER

With a New Covenant, there is also a New Passover. Just like the Passover of the Old Covenant, which God commanded be continually offered, so too does Christ command us to continually be renewed in His New Covenant. Every participation in the Old Covenant Passover was a renewal of God's Covenant.

> *Christ, our Passover, was sacrificed for us, therefore let us keep the feast" (1 Corinthians 5:7 NKJV).*

The Catechism of the Catholic Church describes the Eucharist as, "the source and summit of the Christian life". [37] The Catholic Church teaches that Jesus is truly and substantially present in the bread and the wine of consecration. Even for the most devout of Catholics, let alone Christians who have been brought up being taught otherwise, this can be a huge impediment to the faith.

For Catholics (myself included), sometimes through complacency or lack of faith, similar to the disciples in John 6 who walked away when believing became too difficult, we can underappreciate the miracle of Christ giving Himself to us in this form. Some would suggest that this is really just a symbol,

---

[37] Catechism of the Catholic Church. Paragraph 1324.

a reminiscing of the Last Supper. Some believe the bread and wine really only *represent* Jesus. They interpret the Scriptures to assume that Jesus was speaking figuratively or metaphorically.

In my discussions with my Reformed friends, I couldn't help but ponder the significance of this ritual. Why would it be so important? Why would a mere symbol be the focal point of the Christian Liturgy for two thousand years?

In my own personal faith journey, I approached a crossroads. I felt, like most lukewarm Catholics, that I was not being fed. I began to search for a church and a community that would feed me. I even found some that fed me in certain partial ways such as engaging sermons, contemporary music, modern theatrics, and particular comforts such as coffee, snacks, a relaxed dress code and comfy chairs. I started to see many different Christians worshipping God in different ways. Naturally, this led me to ask what the purest form of worship is.

Before I continue, I do want to make clear, that I believe God can use those exterior things to help draw people closer to Him. Sometimes God works through conversations. Other times He uses someone's book recommendation or video that they shared.

One of my ministry engagements was a non-denominational church that asked me to lead a special event. I happily accept almost any opportunity to share the Gospel. Not everyone would agree with that. However, my mindset is that if God is calling me to share the Gospel, whether it be on the streets to the homeless, at a bar to those who are drunk, or to the complacent in the pews, I will happily follow where God leads.

Throughout my time at this church, I was profoundly taken aback. This special event had the exteriors of something more like a performance. There were stage lights, a fog machine, screens, and booming speakers. There were cinema-style lounge chairs with cup holders. There was a restaurant that served delicious food and snacks, even during the service. In my judgemental mind, I was thinking, surely this isn't what Christ intended the church to look like. My heart began to harden as time went on during this event. What struck me deeply was afterwards, in a conversation I had with the lead pastor. He shared with me how all of this was intentional. They feed hundreds of people every week, many of whom don't come regularly to their church. When he planted this church, most people in their town had stopped attending a congregation. He wanted to do "church" differently. As he started describing this to me, I listened attentively, yet with some hesitation. At first, I felt like it was more of a justification, rather than intentionality.

The pastor shared his vision for a church that was able to capture the attention of the unchurched. He didn't want to fill a room with people who already knew Christ and were part of a church family. He wanted to appeal to people who consider religion as irrelevant and obsolete. He shared with me how he understood that our senses are what initially draw us in and that if people were going to pursue it, at least at first, then it would need to be top-notch.

I began to see where he was trying to go with his vision. What truly changed my perspective was when he referred to his church as a "gateway". He never intended for his organization to be the final destination, but rather a stepping stone into a church family. They were a transition church. This was their identity. The pastor's goal wasn't to grow a flock of his own but to draw in people who would have never given church a second thought, show them Jesus and then point them to a church family of their own. It was never meant to be the end, but rather the beginning.

Even in the Catholic Church, the goal of the faithful is union with God and coming to the fullness of truth. However, we forget that the starting point isn't usually the Mass, the Catechism or the homiletic dissertation of Aquinas. Usually, it starts with an invitation, a coffee, a meal, a conversation, a prayer, a book, a video, a special event, etc. and grows from there. All of these exteriors (music, events, prayers, sermons, etc.) can all be a form of worship offered to God (and should be).

However, on my journey, I kept asking, how are we *meant* to worship God? With all of these practices and expressions, how does God desire for us to glorify Him? Not only that but how has God been preparing us across history to engage with Him? Surely, "church" isn't meant to simply tickle my senses (though that can be used effectively as a starting point). It can't be about what I get out of it. However, this seems to be the criteria for most people when choosing a church. Do I like the pastor? Is the music good? Does it have a children's program? Do they have good coffee? This demonstrates a consumer mentality towards faith, similar to how one might select their preferred foods from a buffet. And upon reflection, I found myself falling into this as well. Though it can be important to draw people in with these externals, the problem is that many stay in that as the "end", rather than the "means".

Is the purest form of worship found in something like singing worship songs? (The musician in me wanted to shout a resounding "yes"!) Is it raising our hands? Is it our service? Is it helping others? Is it fasting, prayer, offerings, tithes or sacrifices?

As I considered what makes up worship, I realized that all of those (and others) are a "form" of worship. However, all of these forms of worship fall short of God's glory (Isaiah 64:6). All of these are flawed and have imperfections. Let's examine salvation for a moment. We are not capable of saving ourselves (Ephesians 2:8-9). It's not possible for humanity (something finite), to mend the rift caused by our sin, separating us from Heaven (something infinite). It takes something infinite and something perfect, something divine, to atone, to bridge the gap. This is why God sent His son Jesus to us, to be that perfect offering, to mend the chasm (John 3:16). So even offering our best in worship still falls short of the worth due to God (Romans 3:23).

The Jews in the Old Testament understood this. They tried to keep the Law of the Torah and offered animals as sacrifices. God used these sacrifices to point to a pure and perfect sacrifice that was to come (Jesus), all the while knowing that these animals could never take away sins (Hebrews 10:11).

If you were a Jew, leading up to the time of Christ, there is one place where you would go to offer a sacrifice for your sins —the Temple in Jerusalem. Hundreds of thousands of animals were sacrificed there, offered to God by a priest. I realized that if I wanted to understand the *New* Covenant that Jesus established for us in the Upper Room at the Last Supper, I must first understand the Old Covenant and how it was to be fulfilled.

This New Covenant was foretold in the prophecy:

> *" My name will be great among the nations, from where the sun rises to where it sets. In every place incense and pure offerings will be brought to me, because my name will be great among the nations," says the LORD Almighty"* (Malachi 1:11).

This prophesy foreshadows not just a sacrifice in one temple, but across the world. It tells us there is going to be a sacrifice that is pure. This implies that everything else does not measure up. At the time of this prophesy, God's people were the Jews. This prophesy would have seemed a bit scandalous. How can a sacrifice be offered for all nations? Even the Gentiles, who do not keep the Law of God, would be able to offer a pure sacrifice to God all across the world, not just in one temple. This concept was an immense stumbling block for the Jews, as is documented in many of the epistles from the Apostle Paul, such as Galatians and Romans.

We see the beginnings of the New Covenant Jesus established, a Covenant that is still celebrated today all across the world, from East to West, foreshadowed in the Old Covenant. This offering, this sacrifice on an altar, is the purest form of worship availed to us. In fact, it is something we participate in. When I realized this, the burden of offering "pure" worship fell off my shoulders. God knows I, myself and unable to offer anything to Him but filthy rags. However, the worship that is offered, is perfect, because it is Jesus, offering

Himself, to the Father, on our behalf. Let's dig into this more deeply by appreciating how it all started.

In the Old Testament, animals were used as a sacrifice to God for atonement of sins. God commanded His people to do this (Leviticus 16:15) knowing they can never mend the rift between Heaven and Earth with an animal sacrifice. However, God used this practice to prepare His people for the pure sacrifice that was to come. In the same way that by choosing sin, death entered the world, God chose to use death in order to restore life. The animals prepared us for that, and Christ's death fulfills it.

Adam and Eve ate from the Tree of Knowledge of Good and Evil, sin entered the world, and God banished them from the garden. However, also present in the Garden of Eden was the Tree of Life, guarded by the cherubim and flaming sword for all eternity. In Revelation 2:7, John writes, "To the one who is victorious, I will give the right to eat from the tree of life". John continues: "To the one who is victorious, I will give some of the hidden manna" (Revelation 2:17). This new hidden manna is Jesus, the tree of life, whom we are to eat.

God has been preparing His people, not only in the way of His sacrifice but also with the way in which He brings His sacrifice to us, as a means for us to renew ourselves in His covenant. Since the time of the high priest Melchizedek, bread and wine have been a recurring theme throughout Scripture. Bread and wine were the first pure sacrifice until it was lost by the Israelites by worshipping the golden calf (Exodus 32), and Jesus reinstated this more perfectly at the Last Supper. Bread is what God used to sustain the Israelites on their journey to the Promised Land—Jerusalem. The new hidden manna is what

God uses to sustain us on our journey to the *new* Promised Land of Heaven.

An important characteristic to note of the Promised Land is that it is a, "land flowing with milk and honey" (Exodus 33:3). The manna that sustained God's people in the wilderness for forty years, was a foreshadowing, a taste of what was to come at their final destination. The manna, the miraculous bread that came from Heaven, tasted like honey (Exodus 16:31).

Interestingly, God's Word is also described in the same fashion, "I took the little scroll from the angel's hand and ate it. It tasted as sweet as honey in my mouth" (Revelation 10:10). God instructed Ezekiel to literally eat God's divine Word, written on a scroll, "Then he said to me, 'Son of man, eat this scroll I am giving you and fill your stomach with it.' So I ate it, and it tasted as sweet as honey in my mouth" (Ezekiel 3:3). Jesus, the Word, the hidden manna, the foretaste of the *new* Promised Land, instituted in a New Covenant, brought about a way for us to be continually renewed in this Covenant, by way of a New Passover.

Not only did God command Ezekiel to literally eat the Word, keeping in mind that John 1 tells us that the Word is God Himself, but we should also note that it tasted sweet as honey. Hebrews 6:5 reminds us that the Word of God tastes good.

With this in mind, Jesus Himself, the Word of God, instructed His disciples to eat His flesh:

* *Our ancestors ate the manna in the wilderness; as it is written: 'He gave them bread from heaven to eat'. Jesus said to them, 'Very truly I tell you, it is not Moses who has*

given you the bread from heaven, but it is my Father who gives you the true bread from heaven. For the bread of God is the bread that comes down from heaven and gives life to the world'. 'Sir', they said, 'always give us this bread'. Then Jesus declared, 'I am the bread of life. Whoever comes to me will never go hungry, and whoever believes in me will never be thirsty. Your ancestors ate the manna in the wilderness, yet they died. But here is the bread that comes down from heaven, which anyone may eat and not die. I am the living bread that came down from heaven. Whoever eats this bread will live forever. This bread is my flesh, which I will give for the life of the world'. Then the Jews began to argue sharply among themselves, 'How can this man give us his flesh to eat?'. Jesus said to them, 'Very truly I tell you, unless you eat the flesh of the Son of Man and drink his blood, you have no life in you. Whoever eats my flesh and drinks my blood has eternal life, and I will raise them up at the last day. For my flesh is real food and my blood is real drink. Whoever eats my flesh and drinks my blood remains in me, and I in them. Just as the living Father sent me and I live because of the Father, so the one who feeds on me will live because of me. This is the bread that came down from heaven. Your ancestors ate manna and died, but whoever feeds on this bread will live forever'". [38]

Jesus' flesh, in the form of new manna that He gives to us, is given to sustain us on our journey to the new Promised Land —Heaven. The new Promised Land, is a place flowing with

---

[38] John 6:31-35, 49-58

milk and honey. Jesus gives us a taste of this Heaven, in His flesh, with the sweetness and goodness of the Word of God. Jesus is the tree of life that the faithful can eat of, to attain eternal life.

This beautiful continuity is also reaffirmed in the Lord's Prayer when Jesus instructs us to pray by asking, "Give us today our daily bread...deliver us from the evil one" (Matthew 6:9-13). The Living Bread from Heaven (Jesus) sustains us on our journey as the Lord delivers us from evil until we reach our final destination—Heaven.

God uses even the simple details throughout Scripture to point to His magnificence and continuity across creation. One small example of this is the place Jesus was to be born, in Bethlehem. The great historian Eusebius of Caesarea points out the small town's significance in the early Fourth Century:

> " *Yes, indeed, I think that it was clearly revealed here that the God of Jacob, from the beginning the Eternal, would dwell among men, and that He would be born nowhere else but in the place at Bethlehem, near Jerusalem, in the spot that is even now pointed out, for there no one is witnessed to by all the inhabitants as having been (349) born there in accordance with the Gospel story, no one remarkable or famous among all men, except Jesus Christ. And Bethlehem is translated, 'House of Bread,' bearing the name of Him Who came forth from it, our Saviour, the true Word of God, and nourisher of spiritual souls, which He Himself shews by saying: 'I am the Bread that came down from heaven.' And since it was David's mother-town as well, the Son of David according to the flesh rightly made His entrance from it*

according to the predictions of the prophets, so that the reason is clear why He chose Bethlehem for His mother-town" (Eusebius of Caesarea). [39]

Mary carried Jesus in her womb to a town called Bethlehem. The word "Bethlehem" literally means, "house of bread" and Jesus refers to Himself as the "bread of life" (John 6:51). Mary carried Jesus, the Bread of Life, to the House of Bread—Bethlehem. She delivered the Bread of Life and placed Him in the manger. A manger is a serving dish for livestock, namely sheep. We recall from the Gospel of Luke's account of Jesus' birth, that the angel appeared to the shepherds. The shepherds were led to the stable to find Christ in the manager. It is fitting that shepherds, along with their flock, adored the Messiah. We are the sheep, and the Bread of Life, Jesus, feeds and sustains us. But surely this is more than just a poetic allusion on God's part.

The Bread of the Presence in the Old Testament Tabernacle, later to reside in the Temple (1 Kings 7:48), was a prefiguring of Jesus present in the bread. God commanded Moses, "Then have them make a sanctuary for me, and I will dwell among them" (Exodus 25:8). God assured Moses, "[There] I will meet with you and give you all my commands" (Exodus 25:22). And finally God said, "Put the bread of the Presence on this table to be before me at all times" (Exodus 25:30), prefiguring Jesus' promise, "I am with you always" (Matthew 28:20).

Jesus draws a direct connection between Himself and the Bread of the Presence, "At that time Jesus went through the

---

[39] Eusebius of Caesarea: Demonstratio Evangelica. Tr. W.J. Ferrar--Book 7

grainfields on the Sabbath. His disciples were hungry and began to pick some heads of grain and eat them... [Jesus] said to them, 'Haven't you read what David did when he and his companions were hungry? He entered the house of God, and he and his companions ate the consecrated bread—which was not lawful for them to do, but only for the priests... I tell you that something greater than the temple is here'" (Matthew 12:1-8). Not only is Jesus alluding to how He is the fulfillment of the Bread of the Presence, but also that this bread is no longer reserved for just the high priest, but is now accessible to all of His disciples.

This "something greater than the temple" is revealed at the Last Supper when Jesus says, "This is my body" (Luke 22:19). In every Catholic Church around the world resides a tabernacle housing the fulfilled Bread of the Presence where God "dwells in [our] midst," where God "will meet [us]," where He "will speak to [us]" and this is how Jesus will "be with [us] always."

We see by just these few examples, how the Word has been preparing us to receive Him in a profound way, since before time.

Jesus made a promise to the Church in Matthew 28:20, "I am with you always, to the very end of the age". We can examine how God has been with us, as documented across history. In the Old Testament, God was present with His people in the Ark of the Covenant. Hebrews 9:3-4 tells us they kept the Law (the Word of God), they kept the rod of Aaron (the authority given to the church), and they kept the manna (the miraculous bread from Heaven). The Ark represented God's presence on Earth. In fact, the bread inside the tent was called "the bread of the presence" (Exodus 25:30). God assured His people, "I [will] dwell in their midst" (Exodus 25:8). Moving ahead to the New Testament, we see Jesus' promise to be with us.

We recognize this presence in various ways. First and foremost in His omnipresence. God is everywhere as the Creator. Figuratively speaking, His DNA is in the fabric of all of creation in a spiritual sense, as at the time of creation, God was a purely spiritual Supreme Being.

Christ is also present in His Church. Believers make up the physical body of Christ (1 Corinthians 12), not merely just as a mystical body. The Apostle Paul affirms for us that Christ and His Church are one, "And God placed all things under his feet and appointed him to be head over everything for the church, which is his body, the fullness of him who fills everything in every way" (Ephesians 1:22-23). When His assembly gathers He is present, "For where two or three gather in my name, there am I with them" (Matthew 18:20).

We see Christ present as "the Word" in the Word, in Sacred Scripture. John 1 reveals that Christ (the Word) is God. The Word which was spoken even before the Incarnation is Christ Himself. When Sacred Scripture is read, Christ Himself is speaking.

Taking after Christ's high priesthood, we also notice His presence in His ministers. In a special way, Christ has delegated His authority to the Apostles and successors, by breathing on them the Holy Spirit (John 20:22) and bestowing this authority on them in the Great Commission (Matthew 28:18-19) and affirmed when Christ stated "Whoever listens to you listens to me; whoever rejects you rejects me; but whoever rejects me rejects him who sent me." (Luke 10:16).

Finally, we recognize that God took on a different form. God, "the Word", took on flesh and became man. He is especially, truly and substantially present with us in a unique way in His body, blood, soul and divinity.

"In the beginning was the Word, and the Word was with God, and the Word was God…The Word became flesh and made his dwelling among us" (John 1:1,14).

I believe that God keeps His promises, and the Word of God has proven this since the beginning of time. So when Jesus says, "I am with you always" (Matthew 28:20), He is going to be faithful to that in a substantial way (in the fullest sense of the word). God being with us, is so much more than simply a mere "spiritual" presence, but the means for our sustenance to the new Promised Land of Heaven.

To more fully appreciate this reality I needed to have a better understanding of how God is with us, His New Covenant that He made in the Upper Room, more importantly, to have a deeper understanding of God's covenantal relationship.

My first step was recognizing Old Testament typology. The Old Testament covenants, sacrifices and even figures such as Jonah, Abraham, Isaac, Moses, Adam, etc. are all types. These are shadows, Hebrews 10:1 tells us, pointing to the fulfillment of them, in the New Testament. For example, Jesus is referred to as the last Adam. The Law was a shadow of the righteousness of Christ. What we need to remember is that the Old Testament prefiguring is never greater than the New Testament fulfillment.

Adam is not greater than Jesus. The miraculous bread from Heaven that fed and sustained the Israelites in the desert for forty years, cannot be greater than the New Testament fulfillment of Jesus, the Living Bread from Heaven, giving His flesh to sustain us on our journey to the new Promised Land—Heaven. The bread of the presence housed in the Tabernacle of the Old Covenant, which was God's presence among His people (Exodus 25:8), is not greater than Christ's presence in the New Covenant when He promised, "I will be with you always" (Matthew 28:20). With this understanding of typology, we can look at how the Old Testament types have pointed forward to prefigure Christ, through God's covenants.

God has created covenants with His people across history. It began with Adam and Eve in the Garden of Eden (Genesis 3), after eating the forbidden fruit and letting sin enter the world, Adam and Eve recognized their sin and shame. They tried to cover their sin with fig leaves. However, God created a covenant with them. He killed an innocent animal to clothe them, to cover their sin.

Abraham waited one hundred years for a son. Finally, after years of waiting, God answered his request only to put Abraham to the test. God asked Abraham to take his son, his only beloved son, up Mount Moriah, and sacrifice him. This is the same mountain Jesus would be sacrificed on hundreds of years later. Abraham's son Isaac carried the wood on his back, up a mountain. Isaac asked his father, "Where is the lamb for the burnt offering?" (Genesis 22:7) and Abraham said, "God himself will provide the lamb" (Genesis 22:8). Just as Abraham was about to sacrifice his son, the angel appeared and told him not to touch Isaac. Immediately, they noticed a ram caught in thorns. We should note the striking parallels between the story of Abraham and Isaac, and God the Father and His son Jesus. Abraham and Isaac sacrificed the ram, and God Himself provided the lamb of sacrifice, in His son Jesus, hundreds of years later, wrapped in a crown of thorns.

Finally, the story which closely resembles our present covenant is the Exodus. The story of Exodus has striking parallels to our present reality. The Israelites were under persecution, and in the bondage of slavery, similar to how we are in the bondage of sin prior to forgiveness. However, God was faithful to His people and told them He was going to save them from slavery. God introduced ten plagues upon Egypt with the last plague being the death of the firstborn. God instructed the Israelites to follow very specific instructions.

The father of the household acted as priest and had to take an unblemished, male lamb, without any broken bones (Exodus 12:5). They would kill the lamb and sprinkle the blood on the wood of the lintel of the door posts with a hyssop branch (Exodus 12:7). They would then sacrifice the lamb (Exodus 12:21). Finally, the family would gather and eat the lamb (Exodus 12:8-11).

There are a few details that helped me to understand the significance of these instructions. This lamb needed to be pure and spotless. In the Old Testament when you wanted to make atonement for your sin, you offered God your best. You didn't give Him the animal that had a limp, was sick, discoloured or disfigured. You offered God your best animal.

When we read the Gospel of John, we recognize the parallels between Jesus, referred to as, "the lamb of God" (John 1:29) and the Old Covenant sacrifice. Jesus was the firstborn male, pure and spotless, "Who knew no sin" (2 Corinthians 5:21). The Gospel of John makes clear that while Christ was on the cross, to fulfill the prophecy, not a bone of His shall be broken (John 19:36).

This parallel chart compares the Old Covenant prefiguring to the New Covenant fulfilment:

Old Covenant	New Covenant
A lamb was used as the atoning sacrifice (Exodus 12:5)	The "Lamb of God", Jesus, died for our sin (1 Corinthians 5:7)
The lamb was sacrificed at three in the afternoon (Exodus 12:4-10)	Christ was sacrificed at three in the afternoon (Matthew 27:46)
The lamb was to be pure and spotless (Exodus 12:5)	Jesus, our Lamb of God was without sin (2 Corinthians 5:21)
The lamb was a male, firstborn and over one year in age, an independent adult (Exodus 12:5)	Jesus was a male, firstborn and independent adult (Romans 8:29)
The lamb couldn't have any broken bones (Exodus 12:5)	Jesus didn't have any broken bones at His crucifixion, to fulfill the prophesy (John 19:36)
The lamb needed to be sacrificed and consumed (Exodus 12)	Jesus was sacrificed and instructed us to eat His flesh (John 19, John 6, Luke 22)
The passover lamb was regularly celebrated (Exodus 12:14)	Our passover Lamb, Jesus instructed us to remember Him (Luke 22:19)
The passover ritual was a true participation in the original Exodus (Exodus 13:8)	In the New Passover, the remembrance of the Last Supper is a participation / "anamnesis" (Luke 19:22)

The blood of the lamb was spread across the wood of the lintel with a hyssop branch (Exodus 12)	Jesus' blood was spread upon the wood of the cross. His last drink of wine was with a hyssop branch. (John 19)
The lamb was sacrificed with two wooden spits, one vertical and one horizontal, making a cross (Talmud)	Jesus was sacrificed on a cross made of wood, one vertical beam and one horizontal beam, a typical Roman crucifixion (Mark 15:32)
The lamb was sacrificed by a priest (2 Chronicles 35:11)	Jesus was both the Priest and the sacrificial Lamb (Hebrews 8:1, John 1:29)
God gave the Israelites manna, bread from Heaven to sustain them on their journey to the New Promised Land (Exodus 16)	Jesus is the Living Bread from Heaven, instructing us to eat His flesh to have life within us on our journey to the New Promised Land —Heaven (John 6)
The lamb was eaten with unleavened bread (Exodus 12:15)	Jesus, our sacrificial Lamb, held up unleavened bread and stated "This is my body" (Luke 22:18-19)

In the Old Covenant, the lamb was sacrificed at three in the afternoon and publicly presented to the people. Jesus was sacrificed on the cross at three in the afternoon (Matthew 27:46) and presented publicly before the world. In the Old Testament, a lamb that was to be sacrificed would have two wooden stakes driven through it, one vertical, through the length of the animal, and the second horizontal, shoulder to shoulder. [40]

---

[40] Babylonian Talmud, Book 3: Tracts Pesachim, Yomah and Hagiga, tr. by Michael L. Rodkinson, [1918], Chapter 3.

Justin Martyr in the early Second Century accounts the Jewish paschal lamb and how it prefigures Christ:

> *That lamb which was commanded to be wholly roasted was a symbol of the suffering of the cross [Greek word 'stauros' which can also mean 'stake' or 'upright'] which Christ would undergo. For the lamb, which is roasted, is roasted and dressed up in the form of the cross ['stauros']. For one spit is transfixed right through from the lower parts up to the head, and one across the back, to which are attached the legs of the lamb" (St. Justin Martyr).* [41]

Justin Martyr describes the image we know well today—The cross. The lamb was affixed to cross-shaped stakes made specifically of wood, as it was sacrificed. So was Jesus, our Passover Lamb. The Jewish Mishna also describes the regulations for the Passover lamb:

> *How should the paschal lamb be roasted? A spit made of the wood...put in at the mouth (of the lamb or kid), and brought out again at the vent thereof" (Mishna).* [42]

The Israelites needed to follow the Passover instructions precisely during the Exodus. If they didn't, they would wake up to find their firstborn dead the next morning. Therefore, to complete this ritual, they had to not only sacrifice the lamb but also eat the lamb. The family would gather and have

---

[41] ANF01. "The Apostolic Fathers with Justin Martyr and Irenaeus", Chapter XL.

[42] Babylonian Talmud, Book 3: Tracts Pesachim, Yomah and Hagiga, tr. by Michael L. Rodkinson, [1918].

communion together. If they completed the sacrifice but didn't eat the lamb (perhaps they didn't enjoy the flavour or didn't consider communion a necessity) their firstborn would be dead in the morning. They had to follow God's instructions precisely.

God freed His people from slavery through the sacrifice of the lamb. He led them into the wilderness on a journey for forty years to the Promised Land. Similarly, once we are freed from sin, we are on a journey also, to the *new* Promised Land, the New Jerusalem—Heaven. God gave them bread from Heaven, manna, to sustain them on their journey. God gives us the Living Bread from Heaven, Jesus Himself (John 6:51) to sustain us on our journey as well.

In the Old Covenant, the lamb was sacrificed publicly for all to witness, but also needed to be applied personally, taken home and consumed—communion with the family. The Israelites needed to apply the blood of the lamb to the lintels of their homes (like we are invited to apply the blood of Christ to the *lintels* of our hearts). They participated in it continually, just like at each Mass we participate and renew ourselves in His Covenant with His blood.

Ezekiel 9:4 tells us, "Go throughout the city of Jerusalem and put a mark on the foreheads of those who grieve and lament over all the detestable things that are done in it". The faithful seeking after God's mercy would mark a "T" on their foreheads, representing the lintel (TAW a Hebrew word, which represents the doorposts from the Passover in Exodus) where the blood was spread. This action was asking for God's mercy, for death to pass over them, just like the Exodus night of Passover. It wasn't just a public display, but also needed to be applied personally.

The Old Covenant had two main parts. First the sacrifice and second communion. They had to participate in the offering of the sacrifice, but also needed to consume that sacrifice. The sacrifice took place, but the blood of the sacrifice still needs to be applied to the lintel of our hearts. How do we do this? By consuming Jesus' body and blood. As I began to see these parallels between the Old Covenant Exodus Passover and the New Covenant, I started to see how similar they are.

However, this one time freeing from slavery that took place for the Israelites in the Exodus wasn't forgotten. It was celebrated regularly. God commanded the ritual as an ordinance for future generations to remember. But more than that, it was also participated in by future generations, and renewed with each act.

God commanded the Israelites, "This day shall be for you a memorial day, and you shall keep it as a feast to the Lord; throughout your generations, as a statute forever, you shall keep it as a feast" (Exodus 12:14). We see similar language in the Gospel accounts of the Last Supper when Jesus instructs His Apostles to, "Do this in remembrance of me" (Luke 22:19).

What is interesting is that as part of the renewal of their covenant, their children would ask the father:

" *What does this ceremony mean to you?" (Exodus 12:26).*

God instructed them to give a prescribed answer:

> " *It is the Passover sacrifice to the LORD, who passed over the houses of the Israelites in Egypt and spared our homes when he struck down the Egyptians" (Exodus 12:27).*

I must have read that passage a few hundred times before the significance took hold. Let's take a moment and consider that statement. Hundreds of years later, the Israelites were "remembering" the Exodus, the great sacrifice that happened at the Passover, once and for all, to free them from the bondage of slavery. But the father, generations later, hundreds of years after the fact, says it is the angel of death that passed and "spared our homes". *Our* homes. Not the previous generation's homes. He, himself, didn't come out of Egypt. He wasn't there in the original Exodus. So what does this mean?

Somehow this father is making himself present, participating in the same Exodus, the same Passover that happened hundreds of years prior. This is the foundation of understanding the Jews had at the time of Christ. Their memorial wasn't a mere recollection or reminisce, but rather a true participation. This was how God's people, the Jews, remained in and renewed their covenant with God.

With this foundation, Jesus instituted the New Covenant at the Last Supper:

> " *Now the Festival of Unleavened Bread, called the Passover, was approaching… Then came the day of Unleavened Bread on which the Passover lamb had to be sacrificed. Jesus sent Peter and John, saying, 'Go and make preparations for us to eat the Passover'. When the hour*

came, Jesus and his Apostles reclined at the table. And he said to them, 'I have eagerly desired to eat this Passover with you before I suffer. For I tell you, I will not eat it again until it finds fulfillment in the kingdom of God'. After taking the cup, he gave thanks [Greek word is "eucharistēsas"] and said, 'Take this and divide it among you. For I tell you I will not drink again from the fruit of the vine until the kingdom of God comes'. And he took bread, gave thanks and broke it, and gave it to them, saying, 'This is my body given for you; do this in remembrance of me'. In the same way, after the supper he took the cup, saying, 'This cup is the new covenant in my blood, which is poured out for you'" (Luke 22:1-19).

There's a lot to unpack in this passage. Firstly, the inspired author sets the tone, letting the readers know that this is in the context of the Passover. If we read this passage through the understanding of a Jew, we would instantly notice something critical. It's a Passover celebration, however, there is no lamb spoken of for sacrifice, and there's no Levitical priest to offer it. Why would this be?

Jesus foretold that He had not come to abolish the Law, but to fulfill it (Matthew 5:17). We see this begin at the Last Supper. He is transforming the Old Covenant into the New Covenant in His own blood. He is both offering the sacrifice and He is the sacrifice. The Gospel of John tells us, "Behold, the Lamb of God [Jesus]" (John 1:29). Similarly, Hebrews 4:14 states, "Therefore, since we have a great high priest who has ascended into heaven, Jesus the Son of God", Jesus is both the priest and the lamb. The Covenant in the Old Testament made with Moses started with, "This is the blood of the covenant" (Exodus 24:8). Jesus quotes this same phrase at the Last Supper, implementing the New Covenant, in His blood. [43]

Secondly, when Jesus says, "Do this in remembrance of me" (Luke 22:19), this correlates to how the Jews would "remember" the original Exodus. Just as God the Father commanded the Israelites to remember, so too is Jesus with the New Covenant. Even though generation after generation had perished, and weren't actually present for the original Exodus that took place coming out of Egypt, they still participated in that same Exodus, through the ritual that God instructed. [44] Even though we were not present at the Last Supper or the cross, we can still participate through the ritual Jesus instructs, in faith and practice. We can renew ourselves in the New Covenant with every act of participation in His New Passover.

When we examine the Scriptures in their native language we can begin to understand how Jesus intended the same practice. The Greek word used for "remembrance" (Luke 22:17) is "anamnesis". Anamnesis means to make something from the past, a reality in the present. [45] It's an act in which "the present is brought into intimate contact with the past" and vice-versa, or more precisely, to "actualize" the past. [46] In Greek culture, anamnesis was a term used to denote the movement of an abstract idea into this material world. In fact, this wasn't a

---

43 Luke 22:19

44 Babylonian Talmud, *Pesachim* 99b

45 Dennis C. Smolarski, *Liturgical Literacy: From Anamnesis to Worship* (New York, NY/ Mahwah, NJ: Paulist Press, 1990), 11.

46 Bruce T. Morrill, Anamnesis as Dangerous Memory: Political and Liturgical Theology in Dialogue (Collegeville, MN: The Liturgical Press, 2000), 177

new concept. Just like how the Jews were able to participate in the original Exodus by celebrating the Passover, hundreds of years later, when God commanded them to keep it as a "memorial", Jesus is instructing us to "remember", to participate. This isn't a mere recollection, reminisce, such as "remember how much fun we had on vacation last year", but a real participation in an event from the past. That past event is being actualized and made present before us in the very moment.

The Hebrew word for "memorial" as used in Exodus 12:14 is "zikaron" and the Greek equivalent of that Hebrew word is the very same phrase Jesus used to instruct us to remember— "anamnesis". Zikaron emphasizes participation in an event of the past rather than simply a mental recollection of that event. The synonymous instruction between these two commands of "remembrance" (Luke 22:17) and "memorial" (Exodus 12:14) is undeniable. In fact, "anamnesis" is used in the Old Testament for sacrificial memorials, in the Greek Septuagint translation. When I became aware of this "making present from the past", it changed my perception of the New Passover.

Today, Catholics around the world participating in the Mass are not making a *new* sacrifice, but are rather participating in the once and for all sacrifice (Hebrews 10:10), that began in the Upper Room at the Last Supper and ended with Jesus' death on the cross. Many times we consider the Last Supper and Jesus' crucifixion as two separate events. When in reality, this sacrifice and sin offering began in the Upper Room and continued with Jesus' death.

Jesus, at the Last Supper, separates His body and His blood, signifying death. His fulfillment had commenced and was accomplished with His death on the cross.

Just like how the Old Covenant Passover lamb was to be sacrificed, consumed, and continually celebrated for its renewal, similarly, Christ our Passover Lamb was sacrificed, He instructs us to consume Him, and every participation is a renewal in His New Covenant.

Now I realize that this was a lot of contrasting verses and far too much Greek. However, circling back to my primary question, of what the purest form of worship is, we come to understand that it's Jesus Himself. Every Mass is a participation in the moment of Calvary. This fulfills the Old Testament prophesy (Malachi 1:11), that from East to West a pure and holy sacrifice will be made among all nations. This is the New Covenant Jesus speaks of in His blood. As I reflected on the historic church, I realized that the only pure sacrifice offered continually, across the globe is Jesus, offering Himself to the Father.

Similar to how the Israelites would remember and be renewed in the Exodus by participating in it, we too participate in the New Covenant, thousands of years later, by making present something from the past—"anamnesis". This is not a re-sacrifice, as Hebrews 9:28 tells us Christ died, "once and for all". Each Mass we are not re-sacrificing Christ, but rather participating in the once and for all sacrifice that took place two thousand years ago. It is a re-presentation of Calvary. We are making the moment of Calvary present to us, by the power of the Holy Spirit, and participating in it, through faith. Just as the Jews would renew their covenant with God every time they participated in the Passover, so too are we by participating in the *new* Covenant Passover.

Many Christians often consider this sacrifice in the past tense. After all, Scripture tells us that it was once and for all, at one point in time. However, Heaven demonstrates for us that this once and for all sacrifice is actually an eternal and perpetual sacrifice, "His works have been finished since the creation of the world" (Hebrews 4:3).

The book of Revelation gives us great insight into the Heavenly Liturgy. John describes Jesus as a "Lamb, looking as if it had been slain, standing at the center of the throne" (Revelation 5:6). Why would Jesus be depicted as a lamb slain? Because He is presenting Himself before the throne in Heaven on our behalf.

Not only is Jesus depicted as a slain lamb, but also as the priest, "Dressed in a robe reaching down to his feet and with a golden sash around his chest" (Revelations 1:13). This is the prescribed dress for the Old Covenant priesthood as well (Exodus 28:4). Jesus, the high priest, is continually, perpetually and eternally offering Himself as the Lamb of sacrifice on the throne in Heaven.

The inspired author of Hebrews also gives great insight into the ongoing, continual, external sacrifice of Christ, presented before God in Heaven:

> *Therefore he is able to save completely those who come to God through him, because he always lives to intercede for them" (Hebrews 7:25).*

> **❝** *And [Jesus] who serves [presently] in the sanctuary, the true tabernacle set up by the Lord, not by a mere human being". (Hebrews 8:2).*

Jesus is continually offering Himself for us. His priesthood is forever, and the expiation of His sacrifice is eternal. This practice of participating in this pure sacrifice fulfills the prophecy of Malachi that, "From where the sun rises to where it sets" a pure sacrifice will be offered (Malachi 1:11).

This can be a hard concept to grasp, I know it was (and is) for me, as Heaven is outside of time and space. Perhaps one way to try and understand this is to think of our material universe as a snow globe. God is eternally outside, looking in on creation. He sees a linear timeline of history from beginning to end, all at once.

The whole Heavenly liturgy is a sacrifice and a communion, a meal, with God's family all gathered together around the same dinner table. This is a family we can only be born *again* into. God is calling His sons and daughters, the church, the bride of Christ, to partake in the family marriage supper of the Lamb:

> **❝** *Blessed are those who are invited to the wedding supper of the Lamb!" (Revelation 19:9).*

As a side note, the Old Covenant Passover gives us a lens into understanding one of the reasons why only Catholics who are in right-standing with God can receive Holy Communion at Mass. Only those who were circumcised into God's Old Covenant (like how Baptism initiates us into God's New

Covenant), and only those who were ritually cleansed, could partake. This isn't some cruel form of rejection by the Catholic Church, but rather a way to protect one from bringing death and judgment upon oneself (see 1 Corinthians 11:29).

I'm sure many can follow the covenantal aspect of God's relationship with us. However, there can still be some disbelief that Christ is truly and substantially present with us in the bread and the wine. It is an outrageous claim if it's true, but after all, Christ did tell us that, "unless you eat the flesh of the Son of Man and drink his blood, you have no life in you" (John 6:53). Holding up the bread He stated, "This *is* my body" (Luke 22:19). Finally He proclaims, "My flesh is true food, my blood is true drink" (John 6:55). Apart from taking the obvious literal nature of His words, let's first back up and examine if Jesus has ever taken on a different form before.

On the Mount of Transfiguration, Jesus appeared with Moses and Elijah and Scripture tells us that Jesus is transfigured before Peter and the other Apostles. Jesus appears to them in a different form (Matthew 17). Jesus does something very similar on the road to Emmaus:

" Now that same day two of them were going to a village called Emmaus...hey were talking with each other about everything that had happened. As they talked and discussed these things with each other, Jesus himself came up and walked along with them; but they were kept from recognizing him... When he was at the table with them, he took bread, gave thanks, broke it and began to give it to them. Then their eyes were opened and they recognized him, and he disappeared from their sight. They asked each other,

*"Were not our hearts burning within us while he talked
with us on the road and opened the Scriptures to us?...
Then the two told what had happened on the way, and how
Jesus was recognized by them when he broke the bread"
(Luke 24:13-35).*

What is fascinating is that the Greek word "aphantos" which
means "to vanish", doesn't imply to depart or to leave. It means
to be made invisible. Interestingly, Jesus didn't depart when He
vanished, but rather, they recognized Him in the breaking of
the bread. The breaking of the bread is the very command that
Jesus gave to "remember" Him, and that the bread and wine
itself is Jesus' body and blood. He remained with them in the
breaking of the bread.

Finally, the most obvious example is when Jesus The Word,
took on the form of flesh (John 1:1,14). Undeniably, Jesus not
only has the ability to but also has a track record of taking on
different forms.

Some might argue that Jesus claims to be "the door" (John
10:9) or "the vine" (John 15:1) and we don't think He is a
literal door or a literal vine. Yet, we believe He is literal bread
and wine, that the substance of bread and wine no longer
remains after consecration, it has changed into the substance
of Christ, and only the outward appearance remains
unchanged. But why? As we've already seen, bread and wine
are a recurring theme throughout the Scriptures. It's not just
mentioned and used as a metaphor one time, such as the door
or the vine, but is used many times. There seems to be a
substantial amount of evidence to lead us to believe that we
should take Jesus at His word, literally when He says, "This is

my body" (Luke 22:19). As we read the bread of life discourse in John 6, we begin to understand Jesus' emphasis:

> *Very truly I tell you, unless you eat the flesh of the Son of*
> *Man and drink his blood, you have no life in you.*
> *Whoever eats my flesh and drinks my blood has eternal life,*
> *and I will raise them up at the last day. For my flesh is real*
> *food and my blood is real drink. Whoever eats my flesh and*
> *drinks my blood remains in me, and I in them" (John*
> *6:53-56).*

Jesus emphatically explains that they must eat His flesh. The Jews are scandalized by this and ask, "How can this man give us his flesh to eat?" (John 6:52). It's obvious that they understood Him to be speaking literally and were scandalized by it, otherwise, what would they have been so upset about? Yet today, many read these same words and only apply them figuratively. Jesus responds next by saying, not only must you eat my flesh but also you must drink my blood. This makes the scenario even more scandalous. Drinking blood is forbidden by the Old Covenant Law. The blood was seen as the life form by the Jews, so it's interesting to note that Jesus says if you want to have life in you, you have to drink His blood.

However Jesus doesn't lay off, He becomes even more emphatic. He states, "Truly, truly" this is important. He states it again. Every time up until this point Jesus was using a word for eat in Greek which means to dine, to consume, like you were going to eat a piece of pizza. However, the last time (verse 56) He changes the word for eat to "trógó", which means to gnaw or chew. This is even more graphic, not the language of someone speaking a metaphor or speaking figuratively. He states, "My flesh is true food, my blood is true drink" (John 6:55). Consider this, if Jesus was really speaking literally (which we believe He was), what else would He have had to say in order to make His point more clear? Nothing. It's plainfully obvious.

Not only that, but Jesus, who knows the hearts and minds, would have known if people were misunderstanding Him. When Jesus is misunderstood in other passages He goes to lengths to explain Himself. For example, In John 3, after Jesus states that we must be born again in order to enter Heaven, and Nicodemus is confused by this, Jesus clarifies.

The end of this passage, in John 6 crystallizes our understanding. It says that many of His disciples withdrew, and they said "This is a hard teaching. Who can accept it?" (John 6:60). It was too difficult to believe. Today many of us struggle with that same dilemma.

If this was a big misunderstanding, why would Jesus not clarify? Why would He let all but His twelve Apostles walk away? If He clarified misunderstandings in the past, why would He not clarify something so scandalous, something that caused thousands of His followers to fall away? What I came to believe is that it's because it wasn't a misunderstanding. Jesus' body and blood are true food and true drink and we are to eat His flesh. How can we know Jesus meant this literally? He says, "The bread that I will give for the life of the world is my flesh" (John 6:51 ESV). If He literally gave His flesh on the cross for us, then in the same vein He intends for us to literally eat His flesh. When He held up the bread and stated, "This is my body" (Luke 22:19), He meant what He said, which is why He commanded us to, "Do this in remembrance of me".

This is how we participate and be renewed in the New Covenant. This is how we abide in Him, by eating His flesh and drinking His blood. The Israelites ate the bread from Heaven to sustain them on their journey, we eat Jesus, the Living Bread that came down from Heaven. If we want life within us, if we want to abide in Him, we must eat His flesh. The only way He gives Himself to us in a substantial way (flesh and divinity) is through how He instructed us to *remember* in the Last Supper. This is what the Mass is all about. This is how we participate in the purest form of worship. This is how we renew ourselves in the New Covenant, just like how the Jews both sacrificed and ate the Passover lamb. This is how we receive our Lamb of God. Upon reflection, I couldn't believe how similar these two covenants were.

In the Old Covenant, the Israelites had to literally eat the lamb of sacrifice. In the New Covenant, we are instructed to do the same, yet many still go to great lengths, at the cost of Scriptural integrity and coherency, to reason that consuming Jesus is merely a figurative practice. God commanded Ezekiel to literally eat the Word of God (Ezekiel 3:1-3). This foreshadowed the Word that became flesh (John 1:14), giving His flesh for the life of the world (John 6:51). If God commands consuming His Word, present in the essence of the ink written on a scroll, how much more will consuming the Word in the flesh profit us?

The Apostle Paul understood this participation as a reality, similar to the Israelites with their participation in the Passover:

" *Is not the cup of thanksgiving for which we give thanks a participation in the blood of Christ? And is not the bread that we break a participation in the body of Christ?"* (1 Corinthians 10:16).

If this was a mere symbol, how can it be a participation in the blood of Christ? Similarly, St. Paul emphasizes the importance of examining ourselves, that if we drink in an unworthy manner we are guilty to the body and blood of the Lord:

" *For whenever you eat this bread and drink this cup, you proclaim the Lord's death until he comes. So then, whoever eats the bread or drinks the cup of the Lord in an unworthy manner will be guilty of sinning against the body and blood of the Lord. Everyone ought to examine themselves before they eat of the bread and drink from the cup. For those who eat and drink without discerning the body of Christ eat and drink judgment on themselves. That is why many among you are weak and sick, and a number of you have fallen asleep"* (1 Corinthians 11:26-30).

If it's just a symbol, why is St. Paul so emphatic? If it's just a symbol, how are we guilty of murder (the body and blood of the Lord)? Why were people sick and dying? Some might suggest that being guilty of the body and blood of the Lord is nothing more than a simple offence, such as being rude, inconsiderate, or insincere. However, St. Paul illuminates for us that the separation of body and blood signifies death, as Christ alludes to in the Upper Room, separating body and blood. When we profane Christ we are guilty of death.

Many are familiar with the secularized Louisiana Voodoo religious practice of poking pins into a doll as a way of cursing another. Though this practice has been Hollywoodized by the media and is greatly disturbing, if one were to violently stab a doll (even a doll in the likeness of another person), would that be considered murder? No, certainly not. The practice would be strange, creepy and disturbing, but not grounds for criminal prosecution. So if I eat bread as a mere symbol, how can I be guilty of the body and blood of the Lord? How have I cast judgment on myself? No such thing would be possible unless this sign made actual what it truly represents—Jesus' presence in the substance of the bread. This is the very nature of a Sacrament.

We sometimes doubt that the bread and wine are truly and substantially Jesus because we cannot see a change with our eyes. Consider when Jesus walked on this Earth. If we were to look at Him, He would have looked like an average Jewish man. If we were to take His blood and examine it under a microscope, would we be able to detect His divinity? No. If the Jews two thousand years ago weren't able to detect with their five senses Christ's divinity when He lived among them, why would we expect any different today from the consecrated bread and wine which He tells us is His body and blood?

The Lord dwelt among His people in the bread of the presence in the Old Testament tabernacle, so also does Christ dwell with us in the Living Bread, in tabernacles across the world, from East to West.

This symbolic ideology that so many modern Christians (including many of my Reformed friends) possess seems to be missing something categorically different from the Eucharist—the presence of Christ in the flesh. One could re-enact the Last Supper as a family or group of friends in their living room, breaking a loaf of bread with grape juice. There could even be a true devotion and sense of unity with Christ through this act (in fact I know many friends who offer this sincerely in their remembrance of Christ's words). But this act would be merely a spiritual communion with Christ. It could be expressed that Christ is "spiritually" present through faith, in the same way that Christ promises that where two are more are gathered in His name, He is with us (Matthew 18:20). What I couldn't understand is if Christ is already spiritually present when we gather, then why would a "spiritual" communion be necessary through bread and wine?

However, this is fundamentally and categorically different from what the Catholic Church would define as "Transubstantiation"—the substance (or essence) of the bread and the wine are transformed (by the power of the Holy Spirit) into the real body, blood, soul and divinity of Christ's true and real self. After all, The New Covenant, at its fundamental core is about Christ giving His flesh and blood for us. Our response is a participation and re-presentation of Calvary's sacrifice. The sign given to us is made actual by the power of the Holy Spirit. The sign isn't simply just a symbol but is made actual in what it signifies.

As I continued to dig into the significance of what Jesus instituted in the New Covenant, I realized that the Eucharist was not the only Sacrament instituted in the Upper Room at the Last Supper.

One seemingly subtle passage we tend to glance over with a quick dismissal is Luke 22:19, *"Do this* in remembrance of me". If we translate that passage from Greek, the transliteration says, *"Offer this,* in remembrance of me". In the Old Covenant, who was ordained to offer sacrifices?—Priests. In Koine Greek, the word for offer is "poiein" and that word is used in the Septuagint translation in various other Old Testament passages to instruct priests to offer sacrifices. One example is in Exodus 29:38, "This is what you are to offer [poiein] on the altar regularly each day" among others as well. We see that Jesus is clearly instituting the twelve Apostles as New Covenant priests, instructing them to *offer* this once and for all sacrifice.

One might suggest that all of us as believers are priests. That is certainly true in one sense, "You also, like living stones, are being built into a spiritual house to be a holy priesthood, offering spiritual sacrifices acceptable to God through Jesus Christ" (1 Peter 2:5).

However, the Apostle Paul distinguishes the priesthood of all believers with what he refers to as the ministerial priesthood, "God gave me to be a minister of Christ Jesus to the Gentiles. He gave me the priestly duty of proclaiming the gospel of God so that the Gentiles might become an offering acceptable to God, sanctified by the Holy Spirit" (Romans 15:16).

Even in the Old Testament, there were three distinctions of priesthood. First, we recognize the universal priesthood, "You will be for me a kingdom of priests and a holy nation" (Exodus 19:6). Secondly, we see a distinction between the "kingdom of priests" and a ministerial priesthood in Exodus 19:21-22, even prior to the Mosaic law (the law of Moses). Thirdly, we see the special role of a high priest who is the only one able to enter into the holy of holies (Hebrews 9:7).

Similarly, in the New Testament, we see these three distinctions of priesthood. We recognize the priesthood of all believers or universal priesthood (1 Peter 2:5). We understand what the Apostle Paul refers to as the ministerial priesthood (Romans 15:16). Finally, we recognize Jesus as our great high priest (Hebrews 4:4-16).

When I overlayed the Old Covenant with the New, I realized what we have is a New Passover, in a New Covenant, with a New Priesthood, with a New Manna, to feed and sustain us on our journey to the New Promised Land (Heaven).

The Last Supper is not the only place we see this priesthood exercised either. In the epistle of James, he exhorts them to call upon the priests (the Greek word "presbuterous") to anoint with oil and pray over those who are sick (James 5:14). The priests are also given the power to forgive sins (James 5:15, John 20:22-23). Why would they need to call the priests for this, if there was no distinction between the ministerial priesthood, the universal priesthood of all believers and the high priest—Christ? Obviously, the ministerial priesthood has a special role, through their ordination.

The Apostles are given this ministerial priestly ordination in a unique way at the Last Supper when Jesus instructs them to "offer" this sacrifice of Him. This ordination follows in a line of succession. The Apostle Paul instructs his successor Titus, having been ordained, to ordain others also. [47] The Apostle Paul also instructs Titus to ordain priests (the Greek word "presbuterous") in every city, just as he himself had ordained Titus.

Saint Paul also instructs Timothy, "For this reason I remind you to fan into flame the gift of God, which is in you through the laying on of my hands" (2 Timothy 1:6) and again in his first epistle to him, "Do not neglect your gift, which was given you through prophecy when the body of elders [presbyters] laid their hands on you" (1 Timothy 4:14).

In John 20:22-23 and Matthew 28:16-20, we read that Christ gave the Apostles authority to complete His work in the Great Commission. He clearly intends for His ministry to continue beyond the initial twelve Apostles when he says, "Make disciples of all nations" (Matthew 28:19). Because it would be physically impossible for them to reach all nations before they perish, this infers that the Apostles must have successors, who can carry out the same tasks Jesus instructed. He is also delegating His authority when He states:

" *All authority in heaven and on earth has been given to me. Therefore go and make disciples of all nations, baptizing them in the name of the Father and of the Son and of the Holy Spirit, and teaching them to obey everything I have commanded you" (Matthew 28:18-20).*

" *As the Father has sent me, I am sending you" (John 20:21).*

---

[47] Titus 1:5

Each Sacred Liturgy of the Eucharist is officiated by an ordained priest. Just like God instructed priests to offer the sacrifice in the Old Testament, so too did Christ instruct His Apostles (and successors) to offer the New Covenant sacrifice (instituted in the Upper Room). Ordination has been handed down by the laying on of hands, in an unbroken line of succession of bishops, who are successors from an Apostle (Acts 1:12-26, 2 Timothy 2:2).

" *Christ our passover is sacrificed for us: Therefore let us keep the feast" (1 Corinthians 5:7-8 KJV).*

St. Paul understood the connection between the Old Covenant and the New. Jesus is our New Covenant Passover Lamb which is sacrificed for us. We are instructed to keep the feast. How do we keep the feast? Meeting on the Lord's Day to break bread, we participate in the once and for all sacrifice from two thousand years ago by participating in the sacrifice but also consuming it.

In every Catholic Church around the world, there are standard regulations and visible expressions of God's presence. Many people might suggest these are simply pious, evil traditions of men, that we should abandon and "just follow Jesus". However, what many don't recognize, as I didn't for so many years of my life, is their Biblical significance:

" *Now the first covenant had regulations for worship and also an earthly sanctuary" (Hebrews 9:1)*

The inspired author points out the particular regulations for divine worship. If the Old Covenant had regulations, what does this imply? The New Covenant has regulations for divine worship as well:

> " *A tabernacle was set up. In its first room were the lampstand and the table with its consecrated bread; this was called the Holy Place. Behind the second curtain was a room called the Most Holy Place, which had the golden altar of incense and the gold-covered ark of the covenant. This ark contained the gold jar of manna, Aaron's staff that had budded, and the stone tablets of the covenant. Above the ark were the cherubim of the Glory, overshadowing the atonement cover... It was necessary, then, for the copies of the heavenly things to be purified with these sacrifices, but the heavenly things themselves with better sacrifices than these" (Hebrews 9:2-5, 23).*

These regulations for divine worship have been preserved in the New Covenant Church, consistent for two thousand years. Most onlookers might assume the various rituals and practices are simply just a collection of traditions accumulated over the centuries. However, it's important to point out that almost every phrase uttered during this Sacred Liturgy of the Eucharist comes from Scripture or is quoted from the early Church Fathers.

Once I started to look, I began to see the obvious Biblical parallels. Sacrifices are offered on an altar, surrounded by candles, golden statues of angels, (Hebrews 9:1-9) and prayers offered to God in Heaven like incense (Revelation 5:8). Priests offering a sacrifice wear vestments, otherwise referred to as robes (Revelation 1:13, Exodus 28:4), just like our great High Priest, Jesus (Revelation 1:13). Just how God instituted various rituals for divine worship in the Old Covenant, Jesus has given us a new set of practices for the New Covenant.

The Gospel of John even uses the Greek word "Eucharistos" or "Eucharistia" meaning to give thanks. This is where the word, "Eucharist" originates. You will recall from the Last Supper, that Jesus after "giving thanks" broke the bread and blessed it (Luke 22:19). The Last Supper was the very first Eucharist of Jesus' body and blood. The Sacred Liturgy was established by Christ Himself and has been celebrated for two thousand years across the world, from East to West, on an altar, unwaveringly. The Sacred Mass is designed to be the medium in which the faithful "give thanks". The gift we receive from that thanksgiving is the sustenance Christ gives us in His body and blood.

The first Christians met on the Lord's Day, the day Christ rose from the dead, to break bread. Some interpret "breaking bread" to simply mean, sharing a meal. I hope by now we understand the significance is so much more than that. They celebrated the Eucharist (the fulfillment of the Passover) because this is how we celebrate, participate, renew and remember the New Covenant—with a New Passover.

66 *On the first day of the week we came together to break bread" (Acts 20:7).*

My original question of *what is the purest form of worship* is answered by the Apostle Paul. He instructs us on how to worship, and what the centre of our worship is. This is how we are to worship until the Second Coming:

> *For whenever you eat this bread and drink this cup, you proclaim the Lord's death until he comes" (1 Corinthians 11:26).*

Up until this point I had examined the evidence from Scripture. However, I really wanted to see what the first Christians practiced. How did the disciples and successors of the Apostles, understand what Jesus spoke?

The Didache is a historical document written around 70 A.D. before the New Testament had finished being written. Scholars tell us it was somewhat of an instruction manual from the Apostles, to the early church. The Didache instructs Christians to:

> *Assemble on the Lord's Day, and break bread and offer the Eucharist; but first make confession of your faults, so that your sacrifice may be a pure one" (The Didache).*[48]

St. Ignatius of Antioch, a Catholic bishop on his way to be martyred, eaten by lions at the Colosseum in Rome, writes within a decade of the last book of the New Testament being written:

---

48 "Didache." . The Teaching of the Twelve Apostles (translation Roberts-Donaldson). N.p., n.d. Web. 13 Aug. 2014.

" Beware of the heretics...They abstain from the Eucharist and from prayer, because they do not confess the Eucharist to be the flesh of our Saviour Jesus Christ" (St. Ignatius of Antioch). [49]

This is what Christians believed for the first fifteen hundred years of Christianity. The Catholic Church is the most ancient of Christian churches, instituted by Christ Himself, and an unbroken line of succession of Popes and bishops traced back to the twelve Apostles in the Upper Room, reassures us of the faith once and for all handed down to the saints (Jude 1:3). If you were a Christian in the first few centuries and didn't believe the Eucharist was the true body and blood of Jesus, you were considered a "heretic"! A thorough investigation of historical records shows that it is hard to find anyone who denies the Eucharist and Christ's presence prior. Personally, I found this extremely compelling.

Even Martin Luther, the father of the Protestant Reformation believed something happened on the altar. He didn't believe exactly in "transubstantiation" (that the substance of the bread and wine transform into Jesus), but rather he held to a doctrine of "consubstantiation" (that the substance of the bread and the wine reside along with Jesus). Nonetheless, Luther still believed in the significance of this Sacrament, and recognized that individualism creates disunity of truth:

---

[49] "Ignatius to the Smyrnaeans." St. Ignatius of Antioch to the Smyrnaeans (Roberts-Donaldson Translation). N.p., n.d. Web. 13 Aug. 2014.

" There are almost as many sects and beliefs as there are heads; this one will not admit Baptism; that one rejects the Sacrament of the altar [The Eucharist]; another places another world between the present one and the day of judgment; some teach that Jesus Christ is not God.   There is not an individual, however clownish he may be, who does not claim to be inspired by the Holy Ghost, and who does not put forth as prophecies his ravings and dreams" (Martin Luther). [50]

Luther goes on to speak specifically on the Eucharist:

" Who, but the devil, has granted such license of wresting the words of the holy Scripture? Who ever read in the Scriptures, that… 'is' is the same as 'it signifies'?…Not one of the Fathers of the Church, though so numerous, ever spoke as the Sacramentarians: not one of them ever said, It is only bread and wine; or, the body and blood of Christ is not there present…. but they are all of them unanimous" (Martin Luther). [51]

We can appreciate the position the early Christians held when we examine their writings:

" For not as common bread nor common drink do we receive these; but since Jesus Christ our Savior was made incarnate by the word of God and had both flesh and blood

---

[50] Martin Luther (cited in Leslie Rumble, Bible Quizzes to A Street Preacher [Rockford, Ill.: Tan Books, 1976], 22).

[51] Martin Luther (Luther's Collected Works, Wittenburg Edition, no. 7 p, 391).

for our salvation, so too, as we have been taught, the food which has been made into the Eucharist by the Eucharistic prayer set down by Him, and by the change of which our blood and flesh is nourished, is both the flesh and the blood of that incarnated Jesus" (St. Justin Martyr, A.D. 100-165). [52]

" *But what consistency is there in those who hold that the bread over which thanks have been given is the body of their Lord, and the cup His blood, if they do not acknowledge that He is the Son of the Creator... How can they say that the flesh which has been nourished by the body of the Lord and by His blood gives way to corruption and does not partake of life? ...For as the bread from the earth, receiving the invocation of God, is no longer common bread but the eucharist, consisting of two elements, earthly and heavenly" (St. Irenaeus of Lyons, A.D. 140-202).* [53]

" *If Christ Jesus, our Lord and God, is Himself the High Priest of God the Father; and if He offered Himself as a sacrifice to the Father; and if He commanded that this be done in commemoration of Himself — then certainly the priest, who imitates that which Christ did, truly functions in place of Christ" (St. Cyprian of Carthage, A.D. 200-258).* [54]

---

[52] "The First Apology." CHURCH FATHERS: (St. Justin Martyr). N.p., n.d. Web. 13 Aug. 2014.

[53] "Against Heresies (Book IV, Chapter 18)." CHURCH FATHERS: Against Heresies, IV.18 (St. Irenaeus). N.p., n.d. Web. 13 Aug. 2014.

[54] "Epistle 63." CHURCH FATHERS: (Cyprian of Carthage). N.p., n.d. Web. 13 Aug. 2014.

" For just as the bread and the wine of the Eucharist
    before the holy invocation of the adorable Trinity were
    simple bread and wine, but the invocation having been
    made, the bread becomes the Body of Christ and the wine
    the Blood of Christ" (St. Cyril of Jerusalem, A.D. 350). [55]

The quotes from the early Church Fathers referenced are
merely a small fraction of testimony provided by the first
faithful Christians. Once again I will say, don't take my word
for it. Read their writings. After all, this is a bold claim. Either
the Eucharist is a mere symbol or it's truly Jesus. I believe there
is an overwhelming amount of evidence to show us this is what
Jesus intended when He gave His flesh to the Church saying,
"This is my body" (Luke 22:19) and "My flesh is true food, my
blood is true drink" (John 6:55).

This is how He remains with us when He says, "I will be
with you always" (Matthew 28:20). If modern Christianity's
practice and understanding of this doctrine changed along the
way (approximately five hundred years ago following the
Reformation), we must ask *why*. We can see that the disciples
who walked on the same soil as Christ, understood what He
meant, they took Him at His Word. This understanding has
been preserved all through the centuries.

For years I resented attending the Mass. Week after week
reciting the same prayers, in the same order with the same
songs. I felt like I wasn't being fed spiritually, which is
interestingly ironic. I have come to realize I was intellectually

---

[55] "Nicene and Post-Nicene Fathers, Ser. II, Vol. VII: The Catechetical Lectures of S. Cyril.: S. Cyril's Writings." Nicene and Post-Nicene Fathers, Ser. II, Vol. VII: The Catechetical Lectures of S. Cyril.: S. Cyril's Writings. N.p., n.d. Web. 13 Aug. 2014.

ignorant of how Christ gives Himself to us, and how at every Mass, we are participating in Heaven. I was resentful and ignorant of a two-thousand-year-old Liturgy whose integrity has been kept consistent, passed down from the Apostles and their successors. No amount of contemporary worship music, lighting effects, hip engaging pastors, comfy chairs, delectable brews, multimedia, or cutting-edge modernized liturgy can ever come close to the gift the Church has been given—Christ truly present with us in His flesh and glorified body, blood, soul and divinity. That should carry a significant amount of weight coming from someone who is a contemporary Christian musician by profession!

That's not to say that those other forms of worship don't have a place in the church. Personal devotions such as prayer through song, and special encounters (conferences and events etc.) are incredible mountain-top experiences that help to inspire a deeper desire for God. However, what I realized is that when we go down the mountain, we need manna to be fed and sustained on our journey. I didn't understand that what I truly desired to fully satisfy me, was Christ Himself. He was right in front of me, but just like those two disciples on the road to Emmaus, my eyes were prevented from recognizing Him.

In closing, we should take note of the prayer that Jesus taught us—the Lord's Prayer. St. Jerome (who translated the Bible, the Septuagint, from Greek into Latin) noticed something striking about this sacred prayer. Jesus says, "Give us this day our daily bread". The English phrasing of this is a bit redundant, "This day our daily bread". Why would Jesus state the same point twice?

However, when we examine the Greek and look at a more literal translation of this passage, we have a better understanding of what the meaning implies. The Greek word used is "epiousios", which Jerome translated as "give us this day, our super-substantial bread". St. Ambrose commented further on what this super-substantial bread is:

> *He [Jesus] called it bread indeed, but He called it epiousion, that is, supersubstantial. It is not the bread that passes into the body but that bread of eternal life, which sustains the substance of our souls. Therefore, in Greek it is called epiousios." (St. Ambrose)* [56]

The Lord gave miraculous bread from Heaven, manna, to the Israelites in the desert for forty years. Every day they were given just enough bread that they needed (and probably got bored of it as well, like perhaps some of us do today). Jesus is the Living Bread, the super-substantial bread that has come down from Heaven, given to us daily, on altars from East to West, from all nations, to sustain us on our journey. Jesus Christ's body, blood, soul and divinity is our New Passover Lamb.

After uncovering all of this I felt both inspired and convicted. It wasn't about my preferences. Many people struggle with the Mass (myself included for many years) because it's boring, perhaps some parishes have awful music or lousy homilies. However, I realized that this mentality is man-

---

[56] Saint Ambrose, De Sacramentis, 5.4.24; English translation from The Fathers of the Church, Saint Ambrose, Washington, DC: CUA Press, (1963).

centered worship, not God-centered. Our worship of God is not meant to edify us but rather is the worth that is due to God.

To remedy this, I looked at practicing the faith from a different perspective. Say if I were a Jew leading up to the time of Christ, it wouldn't matter if I didn't like the taste of lamb, or if I thought Hebrew was boring. It wouldn't matter if I didn't like the sight of blood or the smell. If I desired to be faithful to the way God instructed His people to worship, I had to partake in the Passover. The same applies to the New Covenant. It is Jesus, continually and perpetually offering Himself to God the Father, on our behalf. And through this participation in Jesus' once and for all sacrifice, we are fed and sustained to the New Promised Land of Heaven. God forgive me for all the times I felt Mass was boring. I simply failed to recognize the miracle unfolding before me.

13

MISCONCEPTIONS

One of the most frustrating parts of dialogue is not being listened to and not being heard. It took years of experiencing this to finally realize that not only was I a victim of this but I was also the culprit.

Whether it was the idea that I worshipped Mary, added books to the Bible, invented Purgatory, am being saved by works, call priests "father" when Jesus explicitly forbids it etc. the hardest part was being able to find a listening ear that was truly attempting to understand, rather than regurgitating a sound bite. No matter the misconception, as I would try and explain, "No, I don't worship Mary" (for example), my opponent would quickly follow up with, "Yes, right… but you worship Mary". After continually stating, "No, I don't", I realized that I wasn't being heard (issue after issue).

This was a blessing in disguise as it made me aware of all of the times that I was in discussions with others, but wasn't really listening to them. One of the approaches of apologetics is laying out logical progressions in an argument to lead someone from fallacy to truth. However, what can often happen is that this systematic approach can be used as a tactic instead, leading them into a "got you" trap, rather than an earnest pursuit of truth in fellowship. Too often we settle for hurling sound bites when what might be most effective is simply a listening ear.

I also began to realize that people have many different obstacles and stumbling blocks towards Catholicism. These non-starters come from all angles. Some might reject the faith because of the Papacy, another because of the Mary stuff, another because of a certain Biblical interpretation. Whatever the source, many times the reason for rejection is largely due to a misconception as to what the Church *actually* teaches.

Archbishop Fulton J. Sheen is famously known for saying:

> 66 *There are not one hundred people in the United States who hate The Catholic Church, but there are millions who hate what they wrongly perceive the Catholic Church to be" (Archbishop Fulton J. Sheen).* [57]

This is why we pursue apologetics with love, with the goal of adding illumination to the misconceptions.

CALL NO MAN FATHER

One of the foremost questions I was asked early on is, why do Catholics call priests "father"? Especially in light of Christ's own words:

> 66 *Do not call anyone on earth 'father'"* (Matthew 23:9).

At first, this seems contradictory. Christ was using hyperbole to demonstrate the hypocrisy of the Scribes and Pharisees. Jesus goes on to say we shall not call anyone "teacher". Yet, we

---

[57] Fulton J. Sheen, *Radio Replies*, Radio Replies Press, 1938

see in the New Testament on a number of occasions that the apostle Paul calls himself "teacher" (1 Timothy 2:7, 2 Timothy 1:11). Is Paul contradicting Christ's words? No. What many don't realize is that the Latin word for doctor is teacher. Still, most call professors and physicians by this title.

We can simply ask the question, what do you call your earthly dad? Father. Perhaps a better question is to ponder what Jesus' point was. Did He want us to legalistically outlaw a word that points to the image of divine fatherhood? No. He wants us to give honour and glory due only to God, to God, not to man.

Lastly, if fundamentalists take this passage to the extreme, then it would mean that Jesus Himself broke His own command. In Luke 16:24, Jesus calls Abraham "father", as does the apostle Paul (Rom. 4:18).

What is even worse, is that Paul calls himself "father" in the context of being a spiritual father to those he preached the gospel to:

> *Even if you had ten thousand guardians in Christ, you do not have many fathers, for in Christ Jesus I became your father through the gospel" (1 Corinthians 4:15).*

Further in the New Testament, Stephen calls priests "father" in Acts 7:1-3 as well as John, writing to the "fathers" in 1 John 2:13.

ENGRAVED IMAGES

Another question often given is why Catholic Churches are adorned with images, icons and statues when Scripture says not to make any engraved images.

It would appear as though the Catholic Church is stocked full with the very prohibition of statues that God explicitly commanded in the Old Testament. Isn't this idolatry?

In Exodus, God commands His chosen people:

> *You shall not make for yourself an image in the form of anything in heaven above or on the earth beneath or in the waters below" (Exodus 20:4).*

Does this mean we cannot have visual art, sculptures, carvings or statues outright?

There are two important considerations to this command. Firstly, God Himself commanded images to be made (Exodus 25:18-22, Exodus 26:1,31, Numbers 21:8-9). He instructed His people to place golden angels at the very place of worship. Surely, God can't be outright banning statues, if in just a few chapters, He commanded them to be constructed. The second consideration is that the emphasis lies on the reasoning behind the command. God said:

> *You shall not bow down to them or worship them" (Exodus 20:5).*

This was a precursor to the Israelites' disobedience, when they collected gold from among the people, melted it, formed it into the shape of a calf, and bowed down to worship it.

Ultimately God wants our hearts and desires for us to have Him as the focus of our worship. Idolatry is elevating something else (in Heaven or on the Earth, or under the Earth), above God, bowing to it and worshipping it. Today in Catholic Churches we have art, images and sculptures that depict the moment of calvary (crucifix), the heroic virtue of the Saints (statues) and Bible stories that come to life (stained glass). Though it might be possible to do so, it would seem unreasonable to assume people are bowing down to these plain objects and offering worship to them, in place of God.

These visuals are simply tools to help point us toward God. Similar to how a parent might hold a photograph of their family when they have to travel for work, and even kiss it as a sign of affection for them, so can these sacred pieces remind us of Heavenly things. Giving these material objects the worship due only to God is wrong. However, we are simply using these visuals as a reminder to point us toward Him.

It would be unfortunate to assume that idols can only take the form of images and statues. The Christian community at large is in danger of idolatry of preference, consumerism, worship music, spiritual figures, etc. among other things. Idolatry enters when it detracts from Jesus (or is elevated higher), rather than pointing towards Him.

PURGATORY

When I was still in junior high school I attended a wonderful Baptist youth group. Our small Catholic Church didn't have a youth program and many of my friends attended this one. The youth leaders had a passion for inspiring the faith, a love of Scripture and a desire to lead everyone who came, to know Christ. I am eternally grateful for this season in my life because it demonstrated a people who had a real authentic love of God and willingness to live their faith.

I never felt anything other than welcomed by that Baptist church and still to this day have fond memories of the infancy of my faith life. However, this was one of the first recognizable moments that I remember being challenged in my faith for being Catholic.

As we were in the midst of a small group activity, a Baptist youth from the program turned to me, knowing I was a Catholic, and asked out of the blue, "Why did the Catholic Church invent Purgatory? It's not found in the Bible…".

As a tween, obviously I had no good response to that question other than, "Um, I don't know…". This is sadly, where this misconception tends to stay for most people.

First of all, we must define what Purgatory is and what it is not. There are only two final destinations, Heaven and Hell. Purgatory is not a third option, in addition to these. It's not a second chance for the forgiveness of sins. It's not even a place bound by time necessarily.

The Catholic Church teaches that Purgatory is simply the process of a final cleansing. It's a transition between Earth and

Heaven. Many non-Catholics object to this teaching, citing that there is no Biblical evidence.

It is correct that the word "Purgatory" is not in the Bible. Just like the word "Trinity", or "Hypostatic Union", etc. is not found in the text of Scripture either. However, that doesn't mean the concept is not found in Scripture.

Revelation says regarding Heaven:

❝ Nothing impure will ever enter it" (Revelation 21:27).

Many of my Reformed friends would suggest that our sins are covered by God's grace, so when He sees us, He sees only the righteousness of Christ. However, even if that were to be true, we are still imperfect. We still have attachments to sin. So if nothing impure can enter Heaven, how can we ever expect to get there in our current state? It points to the necessity of some final cleansing or purging of our sins to happen before we can enter Heaven.

This purging can happen on Earth, in fact, if we are striving to lead holy virtuous lives in God's will we should be participating in allowing God to cleanse us.

But even the most holy of Christians, must admit we still fail, miss the mark and sin. If nothing "impure" can enter Heaven, then Christ must purify us completely, before we enter. That final purging is the process which the Catholic Church calls "Purgatory".

In 1 Corinthians 3, Paul tells us that on the Day, our works will be tested as though going through fire (like metals which are purified of their imperfections). If the works survive we will receive our reward. If our works suffer loss, we:

" *Will be saved—even though only as one escaping through the flames" (1 Corinthians 3:15).*

This explains why the imagery of fire is often associated with Purgatory.

Purgatory is only for those who are saved. And to get to Heaven, you have to go through fire to be purified like gold burning away its imperfections.

Simply stated we might ask ourselves the question — Are we perfect now, even after Christ has forgiven us our sins? I know for certain that I am not perfect, even after having received God's grace and mercy. So if that is the case, Scripture proclaims that there is no way for anything impure to get to Heaven. Therefore we can conclude based on Sacred Scripture, the necessity of a final purgation, or cleansing of sin.

Lastly, God is not a liar, He doesn't declare something to be holy which is not. He makes us holy through and through. What His Word sets forth to do, He will accomplish.

INTERCESSION OF THE SAINTS

For many of my Reformed friends, asking the intercession of the Saints in Heaven is a real stumbling block. For many, this would be a non-starter. Personally, I believe this stems from a view of equating "prayer" with "worship". Quite understandably, we are reminded we have only one mediator—Jesus Christ. Shouldn't we just go directly to Him?

" *For there is one God and one mediator between God and mankind, the man Christ Jesus" (1 Timothy 2:5).*

However, Scripture commands us to pray and intercede for one another as members of the body of Christ:

" *I urge, then, first of all, that petitions, prayers, intercession and thanksgiving be made for all people— for kings and all those in authority, that we may live peaceful and quiet lives in all godliness and holiness. This is good, and pleases God our Savior, who wants all people to be saved and to come to a knowledge of the truth" (1 Timothy 2:1-5).*

If Paul is instructing us to only utilize Jesus as our intercessor, is it not a contradiction that three verses earlier he instructs Christians to be mediators for each other as well? James also gives us a similar instruction:

" *Therefore confess your sins to each other and pray for each other so that you may be healed. The prayer of a righteous person is powerful and effective" (James 5:16).*

He goes on to tell us about Elijah and the effectiveness of his prayers because of his righteousness:

" *Elijah was a human being, even as we are. He prayed earnestly that it would not rain, and it did not rain on the land for three and a half years. Again he prayed, and*

the heavens gave rain, and the earth produced its crops"
(James 5:17-18).

James uses Elijah as the ultimate example to display that prayers are more effective when we are asking them in a higher degree of righteousness. Those Saints in Heaven are even more "powerful and effective", as they are completely free of sin and perfected by God.

One might suggest that those in Heaven are separated from us. But are not all sincere Christ-followers members of the body of Christ, buried with Christ in baptism and raised with Him also (Colossians 2:12)? Does this membership end with earthly death? Absolutely not. Our souls are members of the mystical body of Christ. Jesus Himself said,

> ❝ *'I am the God of Abraham, the God of Isaac, and the God of Jacob'? He is not the God of the dead but of the living"*
> *(Matthew 22:32).*

The Apostle Paul reminds us that in Heaven we continue to stay members of His body:

> ❝ *For I am convinced that neither death nor life, neither angels nor demons, neither the present nor the future, nor any powers, neither height nor depth, nor anything else in all creation, will be able to separate us from the love of God that is in Christ Jesus our Lord"* (Romans 8:38-39).

So perhaps it is misleading to describe this practice as, "praying to the dead", because those faithful souls who have perished here on Earth, in God's favour, are not dead, but are truly alive in Christ, perhaps even more fully alive.

If one were to be able to grapple with that, the next obstacle is that those in Heaven couldn't possibly be aware of the things of Earth. However, in Revelation, John makes visible the offerings of our prayers to God:

66 *And when he had taken it, the four living creatures and the twenty-four [presbyters] fell down before the Lamb. Each one had a harp and they were holding golden bowls full of incense, which are the prayers of God's people"* (Revelation 5:8).

The twenty-four presbyters are real beings (deceased faithful, not angels), offering the prayers of the saints (who are the believers on Earth) to God. Prayers are not physical matter, yet John depicts the offering here as incense, indicating to us that the prayers offered to God are through the presbyters. The presbyters are intervening for us as they offer the prayers of the saints (our prayers) to the Lamb. The presbyters have an awareness of earthly things, specifically our prayers, and are interceding for us.

But even if they were not aware of the details of the prayers, does that make their intercession ineffective? I receive prayer requests all the time from people who do not want to disclose what the prayer intention is or even who it is for. Does this mean that my effort of intercession towards these is a wasted initiative? I think not. So why would it be any different for those in Heaven currently interceding for us as Revelation 5:8 demonstrates?

> **"** *I tell you that in the same way there will be more rejoicing in heaven over one sinner who repents than over ninety-nine righteous persons who do not need to repent"* (Luke 15:7).

Surely Heaven is aware of what's going on on Earth. They rejoice over a sinner who repents and those in Heaven are doing what Jesus is doing—continually interceding on our behalf.

Another objection to this practice is that it is necromancy. One might argue that the Bible condemns conjuring up the dead, isn't this the same thing? Often times Deuteronomy 18:10-11 is used to try and prove that God has forbidden conversing with the deceased. However, Jesus Himself had both Moses and Elijah appear with Him on the Mount of Transfiguration. One might propose that this was simply a vision. However, we can quickly disregard this idea by recognizing that the Apostles considered the experience reality by desiring to build three tents for their new guests to reside in. Jesus was also conversing with these faithful deceased, Godly men, along with Peter and the other Apostles (Matthew 17:3). There is an obvious difference between sorcery to conjure spirits in order to predict the future, and asking for intercession.

Some suggest that this is considered a form of idolatry. Sometimes we presume that prayer equates to "worship". However, a closer look at what "prayer" is, clarifies this for us. The word *pray* simply means, "to ask". There are numerous examples of the word pray used in Scripture apart from the action of worship:

> *"And Abram said unto Lot, Let there be no strife, I pray thee, between me and thee, and between my herdmen and thy herdmen; for we be brethren" (Genesis 13:8 KJV).*

> *"And the eunuch answered Philip, and said, I pray thee, of whom speaketh the prophet this? of himself, or of some other man?" (Acts 8:34 KJV)*

Is it considered idolatry to ask your spouse, friend or family member to keep your intention in their prayers? If not, why then would asking the Saints in Heaven, members of the one body, for intercession be any different? Obviously, we are not worshipping these Saints, nor are we bestowing to them any glory, worship or honour due only to the Lord any more than we are committing idolatry by asking our loved ones for prayers. We are simply, "asking", "I pray thee..." which was Shakespeare's infamous phrase.

Both Paul and James instructed the early Christians to intercede and pray for one another, therefore labelling this practice as idolatry or a form of worship seems unbiblical and unorthodox.

Contrary to contemporary belief, this practice is historical, found in the Jewish roots of the Christian faith. Jews even to this day pray to and for those deceased. In fact, opposition to this practice is a recent development.

Found within the Septuagint, the Greek translation of the Old Testament used by both Jews and Christians, we read about Judas Maccabee praying for his deceased soldiers (2 Maccabees 12:38-46). Even if one does not accept the deuterocanonical books as inspired, we must at least recognize their emphasis of importance, as the author of the book of Hebrews references Maccabees for us (Hebrews 11:35), indicating the author himself considered it necessary. We must also accept the fact that these writings were considered authoritative and inspired by the Jewish Church, and Jesus Himself. This orthodox practice is present across history, right from the successors of the Apostles.

Knowing the Saints in Heaven are that much closer to God, holy and free of sin, "powerful and effective" through righteousness, and knowing that as the body of Christ we are not separated by earthly death, but remain living and united in Heaven—Why would we not ask the Saints in Heaven to intercede for us, just like we would ask our friends to pray for us, in addition to praying directly to God?

FAITH AND WORKS

Many of my Reformed friends suggest that Catholics try to "work" their way to Heaven and tend to think of the religion as legalistic. However, after dialoguing, what many of them find surprising is what the Church actually teaches regarding works in relation to faith and salvation.

The Council of Trent clarifies:

“ *If anyone says that man can be justified before God by his own works, whether done by his own natural powers or by the teaching of the Law, without divine grace through Jesus Christ, let him be anathema" (Council of Trent).* [58]

This should put to rest any suggestion that Catholics can work their way to Heaven. Scripture also affirms this:

❝ *For it is by grace you have been saved, through faith — and this is not from yourselves, it is the gift of God— not by works, so that no one can boast" (Ephesians 2:8-9).*

We are saved by grace, through faith. Our ability to even turn towards God and repent is only possible because grace has enabled us to do so. However, this grace doesn't act in isolation. God is the perfect gentleman. He doesn't force or coerce us. He is patient. He extends all the graces necessary for us to turn to Him. However, it does require our response and movement.

Peter at Pentecost, while preaching the Gospel was asked by the assembly, "What shall we do?" (Acts 2:37). His answer wasn't faith *alone*. He answered them by saying:

❝ *Repent and be baptized, every one of you, in the name of Jesus Christ for the forgiveness of your sins. And you will receive the gift of the Holy Spirit. The promise is for you and your children and for all who are far off" (Acts 2:38).*

"Repent" and "be baptized" are verbs. They are action words. This is our response to grace. Some might even call

---

these "works". However, our ability to "repent" or "be baptized" is only possible by grace having first moved within us. God is the prime mover.

A passage that seems to easily be dismissed by my Reformed friends comes from James 2:

> 66 *You see that a person is justified by works and not by faith alone" (James 2:24 ESV).*

I always try to provide a gentle reminder that this is the only combination of the words "faith" and "alone" found in the Scriptures. Even the most devout of Christian friends have tried to argue away this passage by suggesting it is not proving a "saving faith" but rather demonstrating one's faith to others. However, the passage explicitly states, "Can that faith save him?" (James 2:14). The kind of faith James is referring to is not merely a demonstration of faith outwardly to others, but actual real saving faith. And if it is apart from works, it is dead. Works are very much a part of faith. After all, even the demons believe in God (James 2:19). Works are a necessity, but apart from faith, they are of no avail.

In John 15, we are reminded that obedience is wrapped up in our "believing". In order to "remain" in Him (John 15:4), we must keep His commands:

> 66 *If you keep my commands, you will remain in my love"* (John 15:10)

Paul exhorts the Galatians:

" *You are severed from Christ, you who would be justified by the law; you have fallen away from grace" (Galatians 5:4 ESV).*

We can be cut off from God through disobedience. How can one be cut off from something they never had to begin with? We must continually endure and cooperate with grace.

This is vividly brought to life when Jesus tells the parable of the unforgiving servant, likening it to the Kingdom of Heaven:

" *Then Peter came to Jesus and asked, 'Lord, how many times shall I forgive my brother or sister who sins against me? Up to seven times?'. Jesus answered, 'I tell you, not seven times, but seventy-seven times. Therefore, the kingdom of heaven is like a king who wanted to settle accounts with his servants. As he began the settlement, a man who owed him ten thousand bags of gold was brought to him. Since he was not able to pay, the master ordered that he and his wife and his children and all that he had be sold to repay the debt. At this the servant fell on his knees before him. 'Be patient with me,' he begged, 'and I will pay back everything.' The servant's master took pity on him, canceled the debt and let him go. But when that servant went out, he found one of his fellow servants who owed him a hundred silver coins. He grabbed him and began to choke him. 'Pay back what you owe me!' he demanded. His fellow servant fell to his knees and begged him, 'Be patient with me, and I will pay it back.' But he refused. Instead, he went off and had the man thrown into prison until he could pay the debt. When the other servants saw what had happened,*

they were outraged and went and told their master
everything that had happened. Then the master called the
servant in. 'You wicked servant,' he said, 'I canceled all that
debt of yours because you begged me to. Shouldn't you have
had mercy on your fellow servant just as I had on you?' In
anger his master handed him over to the jailers to be
tortured, until he should pay back all he owed. This is how
my heavenly Father will treat each of you unless you forgive
your brother or sister from your heart" (Matthew
18:21-35).

The servant was forgiven a debt that he wouldn't have been able to pay back in many lifetimes, yet he was reluctant to forgive a fellow servant with a proportionately minor and insignificant debt. The master places this reluctant servant's original debt back on him. He was forgiven, and because of his works, had his debt added back onto him. He spends eternity paying back every cent in prison. What we do, and what we willfully neglect to do, is our response to grace (not faith alone).

Jesus Himself tells us how we will be judged at the end of time. In Matthew 25, the criteria for being welcomed into Heaven is not "faith alone", but rather what we did in response to faith. Did we feed the hungry? Did we clothe the naked? Did we give to the thirsty?

These works don't merit salvation in and of themselves. We can't earn our way to Heaven. No amount of works can repay the debt we owe to sin. That's why Jesus came to be our perfect atoning sacrifice. His grace and our faith in Christ enable us to enter into this relationship. Not works. However, man is justified "not by faith alone" (James 2:24). My Reformed friends like to be adamantly opposed to the idea that works have anything to do with salvation, all the while admitting that works will naturally flow from authentic faith. On this point, we definitely agree.

THE MARY STUFF

If someone were to be able to overcome those common obstacles there is still one giant elephant in the room—Mary. In my travels, the Mary dilemma seems to be one of the biggest sticking points and stumbling blocks for Christians. Don't Catholics worship her? How can she be the source of salvation? How could she be sinless? How could she be ever-virgin? Doesn't the Bible mention brothers and sisters of our Lord? Why do Catholics think she was assumed into Heaven? Sure, she's the mother of Jesus the man, but she can't be the mother of God!

These questions (and so many more) are like a can of worms. They might seem intimidating at first, but rest assured there are some amazing resources to explain why the Catholic Church professes all she does surrounding the Marian dogmas. One noteworthy resource is a book by Catholic Answers apologist Tim Staples entitled, "Behold Your Mother". Staples gives thorough, yet easily communicable answers to these Marian obstacles.

I'm not going to attempt to answer two millenniums' worth of Marian dogmas in this brief chapter, however, I will try and settle some of the simple misconceptions.

I can understand how it might sound blasphemous to suggest that Mary be the source of salvation or that she was necessary for salvation. In stating such, we don't credit Mary's merit, apart from the grace God bestowed to enable this in the first place. God chose Mary to be the sacred vessel through which He chose to come to us. Through Mary, Salvation entered the world. It extends to count Mary as necessary for Salvation. This isn't to say that God couldn't have saved humanity any other way. However, He chose Mary as the avenue to bring the Messiah to us, thus rendering her participation as necessary for salvation. It would be similar to the cross as being necessary for salvation:

> *Having canceled the charge of our legal indebtedness, which stood against us and condemned us; he has taken it away, nailing it to the cross" (Colossians 2:14)*

The infinite God could have chosen to save us in any way. Yet, He chose to be born of Mary and to suffer the consequences of our sin on the cross. They are necessary because He chose for them to be.

Why does the Catholic Church refer to Mary as the "Mother of God"? Simply because Scripture does:

> *But why am I so favored, that the mother of my Lord should come to me?" (Luke 1:43).*

Elizabeth recognized who was in Mary's womb, and thus declared who Mary is, "the mother of [our] Lord". If we want to know who Mary is, we need to understand who Jesus is. The first few centuries of Christianity wrestled with the nature of Christ. Ultimately, the Councils of Nicea [59] and Constantinople [60] decreed that Christ is both fully God and fully man. If Mary gave birth to Jesus, she gave birth to His human nature and divine nature. God used Mary as a unique and powerful way to come to us.

Not only is Mary the mother of Jesus, but she is also our mother as well. This might seem odd to suggest but two particular Scripture passages made this idea solidify for me. First, at the cross, Jesus gave Mary to John:

" *When Jesus saw his mother there, and the disciple whom he loved standing nearby, he said to her, 'Woman, here is your son,' and to the disciple, 'Here is your mother.' From that time on, this disciple took her into his home" (John 19:26-27).*

As the historical text of the Protoevangelium of James [61] alludes, Joseph was an older man when he took Mary under his care in a betrothal. Joseph was no longer alive when Christ died on the cross. Therefore, Christ entrusted her care to John (and in doing so as an extension to the church) as our mother as well.

This isn't compelling to many people. It wasn't for me either for a long time, as it took me years of reflection to begin to extrapolate a deeper meaning from this passage. However,

---

[59] The First Council of Nicaea, A.D. 325

[60] Sixth Ecumenical Council, Constantinople III A.D. 681

[61] Ehrman, Bart D. (2003). <u>Lost Scriptures: Books that Did Not Make It into the New Testament</u>. Oxford University Press

what hit me right between the eyes was John seeing Mary in Heaven in Revelation. As John describes the Ark of the Covenant (Revelation 11:19) now in Heaven, the next thing we see is:

> *A great sign appeared in heaven: a woman clothed with the sun, with the moon under her feet and a crown of twelve stars on her head. She was pregnant and cried out in pain as she was about to give birth… She gave birth to a son, a male child, who "will rule all the nations with an iron scepter." And her child was snatched up to God and to his throne. The woman fled into the wilderness to a place prepared for her by God… Then the dragon was enraged at the woman and went off to wage war against the rest of her offspring —those who keep God's commands and hold fast their testimony about Jesus" (Revelation 12:1-17).*

The Catholic Church teaches that Mary was assumed into Heaven. Not that she ascended there on her own power, but was brought up into Heaven. This might sound foreign, but it's not the first time God assumed someone into Heaven. Both Elijah and Enoch were taken up into Heaven.

> *Elijah went up to heaven in a whirlwind" (2 Kings 2:11).*

The book of Hebrews describes Enoch being taken up as well:

> *By faith Enoch was taken from this life, so that he did not experience death: 'He could not be found, because God had taken him'" (Hebrews 11:5).*

In Revelation 12, John describes the woman in Heaven with all of her bodily features. If she wasn't assumed to Heaven bodily, she would be described as the "souls" of the other saints (without bodies). Not to mention that while history preserved these numerous holy places where these Biblical events took place, oftentimes building churches on top of them so that future generations would know the incredible power God demonstrated when He walked the Earth, we don't seem to have one for Mary's body. We have the various places of the Apostles, the tomb of Christ, the place of His crucifixion, and even the cloth He was buried in. Yet, we have nothing of the most blessed among all women.

There is only one woman who gave birth to Jesus—Mary. And the "rest of her offspring" are all those who "keep God's commands and hold fast their testimony about Jesus" (Revelation 12:17). If we keep God's commands, then Jesus' mother is our mother. Mary is our mother and she is in Heaven praying and interceding for us, to her beloved son.

But how could Mary have been created free of sin? Romans 3:23 states, "For all have sinned and fall short of the glory of God". Surely, there are exceptions to this. First and foremost, Jesus. Secondly, both Adam and Eve were created free of sin (they sinned later). Thirdly, the context of the passage refers to personal sins committed, not original sin. Therefore, this opens up all sorts of exceptions such as children below the age of reason. Mary herself recognized she was in need of a Saviour,

"My soul glorifies the Lord and my spirit rejoices in God my Savior (Luke 1:46).

The early Church Fathers draw a direct parallel between Eve, and Mary as the "New Eve". St. Justin Martyr in the early Second Century makes this bold statement, which is echoed across the ages:

> " *For Eve, who was a virgin and undefiled, having conceived the word of the serpent, brought forth disobedience and death. But the Virgin Mary received faith and joy, when the angel Gabriel announced the good tidings to her that the Spirit of the Lord would come upon her, and the power of the Highest would overshadow her: wherefore also the Holy Thing begotten of her is the Son of God; and she replied, 'Be it unto me according to thy word.' And by her has He been born, to whom we have proved so many Scriptures refer, and by whom God destroys both the serpent and those angels and men who are like him; but works deliverance from death to those who repent of their wickedness and believe upon Him" (St. Justin Martyr).* [62]

Just as Eve was the mother of all living, Mary is the mother of all those who live in Christ. Just as Eve was created free of sin, so too was Mary.

This promise of a new Eve goes right back to the fall of man in the Garden of Eden. As God brings justice to Adam and Eve's disobedience, He promises to put enmity between Satan and

---

[62] St. Justin Martyr, Dialogue with Trypho, c. 160 AD.

"the woman". "The woman" can be none other than the one God chose to bring salvation to the world through:

> *And I will put enmity between you and the woman, and*
> *between your offspring and hers; he will crush your*
> *head, and you will strike his heel" (Genesis 3:15).*

In order for there to be true enmity between Satan and the woman, it would mean that Mary would not fall into sin whatsoever. The devil would never have a hold on her. She was preserved from the stain of original sin, and God extended a special grace to preserve her from personal sin.

The metaphor often used to describe this reality in Catholic apologetics is that of falling into a pit. Someone could have the misfortune of finding themselves having fallen into a deep well that they would not be able to escape themselves. It's not until a saviour comes to rescue them from this pit that they find salvation. However, a saviour could save that person another way. They could warn them of this hazard before they find themselves trapped. The latter example is how the Catholic Church considers God's special saving grace of Mary. God simply preserved her from sinning. It wasn't something Mary merited in and of herself, but by the grace of God.

It was fitting that Jesus came to us, untainted and unstained from anything impure and imperfect. This leads to another parallel—Mary as the new Ark.

The Ark of the Old Covenant housed the very presence of God on Earth. Inside contained the tablets of the Ten Commandments (the Law and Word of God), the rod of Aaron (the Magisterium of the church), and the manna (miraculous bread from Heaven).

At the Incarnation, Mary became the Ark of the New Covenant. She housed Jesus, the Word of God, who would rule with all authority, the true Living Bread that has come down from Heaven. The Old Testament Ark was made of the purest gold. Because it was perfect, if one were to touch it, they would die (in fact this event is described for us in 2 Samuel 6:6-7). Scripture makes obvious the parallels between these two Arks.

In the Old Testament, the Ark was "overshadowed" by God (Exodus 40:34-35), and Mary was overshadowed by God (Luke 1:35). The Old Testament Ark was made of the purest of pure golds. What does that imply if Mary is the new Ark? In the Old Testament, David said, "How can the ark of the LORD ever come to me?" (2 Samuel 6:9). Elizabeth said to Mary, "But why am I so favored, that the mother of my Lord [Ark] should come to me?" (Luke 1:43). The Old Testament Ark remained in the hill country of Judea for three months (2 Samuel 6:11). Mary remained with Elizabeth in the hill country of Judea for three months (Luke 1:56). In the Old Testament when David approached the Ark he shouted out and danced and leapt for joy in front of the Ark (2 Samuel 6:16). He was wearing an ephod, the clothing of a priest. When Mary, the Ark of the New Covenant, approached Elizabeth, John the Baptist leapt in his mother's womb (Luke 1:41). John was from the priestly line of Aaron. Both leapt and danced in the presence of the Ark.

If Mary is the New Covenant Ark, how much more perfect and fitting must she be for her womb to be God's dwelling place?

Lastly, the most compelling passage of Scripture that made this all so clear to me was from the Gospel of Luke when the angel called out to Mary, "Hail, full of grace" (Luke 1:28 DRB). Other translations miss the mark on portraying this bold statement. "Greetings, highly favoured one" (referring to Mary) is close but doesn't quite communicate her unique role. The angel is greeting Mary as "full of grace", calling her that as a title.

The phrase, "kecharitōmenē" (full of grace) is, as Baptist Greek scholar A.T. Robertson writes:

> " *Perfect passive participle of charitoo and means endowed with grace (charis), enriched with grace as in Ephesians. 1:6 … The Vulgate gratiae plena 'is right, if it means 'full of grace which thou hast received'; wrong, if it means 'full of grace which thou hast to bestow'"* (Robertson). [63]

Fundamentally, grace does twofold. Firstly, it saves us. Secondly, it enables us to be holy, without sin. Mary is titled, "full of grace" in the perfect passive tense. Meaning, that a one-time past event has perfectly and perpetually rendered her in a state of "fullness of grace". This might be difficult for those in the English language to understand as our grammar doesn't have such distinctions of tense.

Luke 1:28 doesn't merely imply sinlessness. Rather, it explicitly states, that Mary is in a state, perpetually from a perfect completed act in the past, of fullness of grace.

---

[63] (*Word Pictures in the New Testament*, Nashville: Broadman Press, 1930, six volumes, Vol. II, 13)

" It is permissible, on Greek grammatical and linguistic grounds, to paraphrase kecharitomene as completely, perfectly, enduringly endowed with grace" (Blass, Friedrich, and Albert DeBrunner). [64]

" Kecharitomene, the perfect passive participle, shows a completeness with a permanent result. Kecharitomene denotes continuance of a completed action" (H. W. Smyth). [65]

No matter how the text is rendered from Greek, in either case, God's grace was perfectly and completely endowed to Mary from a past event. Not only that but she was titled as this perfect encapsulation of grace just like Jesus was titled "Prince of Peace" (among other titles).

In my discussions with my Reformed friends, they would often want to suggest that Mary being "full of grace" can't mean she's perfected for all time since others such as Stephan are called "full of grace" as well (Acts 6:8).

Once again, however, the problem is the English translation. The Greek phrase used for Stephan is "charitos", not "kecharitomene". His being "full of grace" was not perfect passive, but rather present tense.

If one is perfectly and completely endowed with God's grace from a past event, there cannot be sin. To suggest this doesn't imply sinlessness is to negate the text.

---

[64] Blass, Friedrich, and Albert DeBrunner. *A Greek Grammar of the New Testament and Other Early Christian Literature.* Translated and revised by Robert W. Funk. Chicago: University of Chicago Press, 1961.

[65] (H. W. Smyth, Greek Grammar[Harvard Univ Press, 1968], p. 108-109, sec 1852:b; also Blass and DeBrunner, p. 175)

Another element of Mary that seems difficult for many modern Christians to grapple with is her perpetual virginity. However, even the Reformers didn't have difficulty with this matter. Martin Luther writes:

> *Christ, our Savior, was the real and natural fruit of Mary's virginal womb.. This was without the cooperation of a man, and she remained a virgin after that" (Martin Luther).* [66]

Among the other Marian dogmas, the fact of her perpetual virginity has been long held across the ages. Going back to the Protoevangelium of James, we are told that Mary was a consecrated virgin, offered in the temple. [67] Lastly, if we circle back to Mary as the Ark of the New Covenant we are reminded that the Old Testament Ark was not to be defiled by man. What then does this imply about Mary as the new Ark?

Some fundamentalist Christians often suggest that because certain places in Scripture describe the "brothers and sisters" of the Lord, they must be Mary's offspring, thus concluding she could not have been perpetually virgin.

I won't address the numerous passages specifically, but each one essentially boils down to a couple of important distinctions.

The Greek word "adelphos", which is often translated as "brother" can mean several types of relationships such as

---

[66] *Luther's Works*, eds. Jaroslav Pelikan (vols. 1-30) & Helmut T. Lehmann (vols. 31-55), St. Louis: Concordia Pub. House (vols. 1-30); Philadelphia: Fortress Press (vols. 31-55), 1955, v.22:23 / *Sermons on John*, chaps. 1-4 (1539)

[67] Alexander Walker. From Ante-Nicene Fathers, Vol. 8. Edited by Alexander Roberts, James Donaldson, and A. Cleveland Coxe. (Buffalo, NY: Christian Literature Publishing Co., 1886.)

cousins, nephews, or even someone who has something in common socially. Lot is called Abraham's "brother" (Genesis 14:14). However, in reality, he was Abraham's nephew. Similarly, Jacob is called "brother" of his uncle Laban (Genesis 29:15). Ancient dialects didn't have words of distinction for these various relationships, so instead of saying, "my father's brother's son", they would simply say, "adelphos", which could mean cousin, or brother or uncle, etc.

Since ancient texts indicate that Joseph was a widow and had a family before Mary. The other "brothers" could quite plausibly be Jesus' half-siblings from Joseph. However, what is quite striking is the absence of these brothers at the cross.

If Mary did give birth to other children, then where are Jesus' brothers and sisters at the cross? Why did Jesus give His mother to John (not one of his brothers, if he had any) calling John "son"?

Something that I must have read hundreds of times and never noticed was how Mary responded to the angel's announcement that she would bear a son:

❝ You will conceive and give birth to a son" (Luke 1:31).

It would be reasonable to assume this makes logical sense since she is betrothed to Joseph. Just like eventually she would be married to him, she would eventually conceive and bear a child. However, this is puzzling news to Mary. She responds by saying:

> **"** *'How will this be,' Mary asked the angel, 'since I am a virgin?'" (Luke 1:34).*

Her response doesn't make any sense unless she was a consecrated virgin. I'm sure the angel didn't need to explain basic reproductive biology to Mary. She simply couldn't comprehend how she, a consecrated virgin, would bear a child. It was the Holy Spirit who made this possible in an extraordinary way.

Yet still, my Reformed friends would cite passages such as Matthew 1:25, "But he did not consummate their marriage *until* she gave birth to a son". They suggested that since the word "until" is used, it implies that after she bore a son, they would have relations. There are two important considerations. First, the prophecy that Matthew is emphasizing is that Jesus is the Christ because he was born of a virgin. He's driving home the point that Mary and Joseph didn't have relations *before* Jesus' birth, therefore demonstrating that Jesus is the Messiah promised of old. Secondly, just because the word "until" is used, doesn't speak to what happened after. A couple of examples from Scripture help us to realize this:

> **"** *As for Michal daughter of Saul, she had no child until the day of her death" (2 Samuel 6:23 LSV).*

Would this mean that after her death she had children? I think not. Similarly, Jesus says:

" *I am with you always, until the end of the age"*
(Matthew 28:20 NAB).

Is God not with us after the end of the age as well? Of course, He is. "Until" only speaks to what is leading up to the event, not what happens after.

There are centuries of writings from Church Fathers speaking to these Marian dogmas. They aren't new or recently invented. As Elizabeth exclaimed of Mary, "Blessed art thou among women, and blessed is the fruit of thy womb" (Luke 1:42 KJV). As Mary prophesies, "From now on all generations will call me blessed" (Luke 1:48).

" *The veneration of Mary is inscribed in the very depths of the human heart" (Martin Luther).* [68]

In the Ten Commandments, we are instructed to "Honor your father and your mother" (Exodus 20:12). Jesus kept this command (as He perfectly kept the entire Law). If Mary is our mother also, so too must we honour her.

My frustration of not being heard prevented many dialogues from being fruitful. I'm constantly reminded of the words of the Greek Epictetus, "We have two ears and one mouth so that we can listen twice as much as we speak". [69] It is in listening to one another that we can more readily answer the deepest doubts and concerns masked in misconception.

---

[68] Martin Luther, Sermon, September 1, 1522

[69] Epictetus. A.D. 60

No matter the obstacle, when we look at what the first Christians believed, and how they understood the Word of God, we can rest assured in the fullness of truth passed down to us.

14

CONCLUSION

This book was never meant to be a complete defence of the Catholic faith. Far from it. With the brief overview of some of the common apologetics, I've only scratched the surface. This is not meant to be "us" vs. "them", Protestants vs. Catholics. This is simply an account of a journey. I truly believe we can learn from each other and grow in our relationship with Christ. I for one haven't got it all figured out. There are perhaps even notions in this book in which I've erred or communicated poorly. If that turns out to be true, I apologize. At the same time, this merely reiterates the fact that I am a work in progress. We are all a work in progress, by the grace of God, journeying towards Heaven and the fullness of truth.

You don't have to be a musician (like me) to share the hope you have in you. These opportunities are all around us. They are found in our workplaces, schools, communities, families and parishes. Let us have eyes to see these moments God places before us, especially in the most unsuspecting ways, such as a stranger we meet on a park bench, or an estranged family member over Thanksgiving dinner. When we start to hear the resounding truths, as we tug on each thread of doubt on our quest toward the fullness of truth, we see that God is faithful. He is patient and is leading us to go deeper. My prayer each day is, "Lord, open my eyes to see the opportunities you place before me today, to bring my faith to the world".

People approach Catholicism from different perspectives and with different hesitations. For some, the Eucharist seems improbable to conceive, for others the Marian dogmas are a non-starter. The good news is that there are plenty of excellent resources available to explain any one particular issue. That's not the heart of my intent here.

As I reflect back on my own journey, I've come to realize that the Lord has led me through that struggle, so I can sympathize with others who are wrestling with those same dilemmas. Furthermore, I'm so grateful to Him, for reproving and correcting my ill-intentions, malice and pride. For many years my heart was overwhelmingly concerned with winning an argument and being "right", rather than an honest pursuit towards the fullness of truth.

Because I've been the villain of the story, and because I've been the victim, as I'm sure many of us have through triumphalism and condescension, I know all too well what not to do. Those types of interactions make for popular and entertaining content on YouTube videos but rarely bear fruit in our real-life encounters. If we don't approach apologetics with love, gentleness and reverence, then why are we even doing it?

To this day, when the occasion arises, I'm still tempted to go into battle with my weapons yielded, with my armour bound tightly, ready to destroy my enemy. What I have to constantly remind myself is that, those whom I consider the villain, Christ died for. Christ longs for them to know the truth. Christ suffered for them. And if He did, so must I. I have to constantly remind myself to sheath my sword, lower my shield and walk out onto the battlefield like a short, four-foot-tall, wrinkly, old nun (Mother Teresa) and with the gentlest of all humility, embrace that beloved child of God, and journey with them through the mines and battlefield.

That doesn't mean, not being equipped with answers. However, it emphasizes our reverence and understanding of the person and their struggle, hesitations, and misconceptions, giving them the benefit of the doubt with all patience, like our Heavenly Father who is so patient with us.

What I have found time and time again, is that when people truly encounter Christ (even Christ through you and me), when they are truly part of a community that loves them right where they are and promises to journey with them, no matter how long it takes, those hesitations toward the faith seem to fade away.

> **❝** *To convert somebody, go and take them by the hand and guide them"* *(St. Thomas Aquinas)*

Perhaps you have felt at one time or another, that you don't know how to answer a particular question about the faith. What took me far too long to realize is, that is ok. This is actually an opportunity to not only learn for ourselves a deeper understanding of the fullness of truth but also to journey alongside someone else.

When we approach these gaps in knowledge with humility, it strengthens the bond of trust in relationships with those we are companioning. Though I am constantly in awe of the Scriptural, ecclesiological and historical brilliance of theologians such as Scott Hahn and Peter Kreft, not everyone needs to have that vast of a database of understanding. We simply just need to know where to find the information and be willing to pursue it with those we have committed to love and serve. Simply responding with, "That is a really good question, and I'm not sure exactly how to explain that, but I'd love to dig into this with you. Let's go examine this together…", bridges our openness to seek after truth, while recognizing our own personal intellectual limitations.

I'd invite you to try something both simple and profound as we walk with others toward truth. As we ask God to open our eyes to the opportunities He places before us (whether a friend, coworker, family member, stranger on the street, or some other interaction that unfolds), pray that the Holy Spirit will give us courage. Let us ask God for extra grace to have the "yes" of Mary, to be used in such a magnificent way, that God might work through us as well. Let us strive to emulate the virtues of patience, generosity, and charity towards those who are sincerely seeking a deeper connection with God. Lastly, let us get out of the way, and put our pride and ego in check, so that God's power might be made perfect through our weakness (2 Corinthians 12:9).

When I started to see what the first Christians believed and how they practiced their faith, everything began to fall into place. Once I discovered that right from the beginning the central form of worship was the Eucharist, that the hierarchy of the Church was passed down from the Apostles, that this living Church is who wrote and preserved the Word of God, all my other hesitations faded. If this is what Christianity believed for a millennium before there became disagreement, why would I follow anything else? Furthermore, all the little hang-ups I had (whether theological tenets or moral issues) seemed to be resolved. If the Apostles handed this down from Christ, who am I to deter?

Once the foundation was in place, all the other pieces began to fall into place. If the early Christians recognized Peter as Pope, then so must I. If the early Christians submitted to the infallible authority of the councils of bishops, so must I. If the early Christians held to a certain Canon and didn't believe in sola scriptura, then I must follow suit....

My criteria for discovering the ancient Church was to simply look at what the first Christians believed as passed down in the Word of God.

There is plenty of great exegesis out there to prove any desired outcome of a passage of Scripture. However, when we change the lens of that issue (whether infant Baptism, Mary, Purgatory, the Pope, etc.), and look through the eyes of the first Christians, the answer is usually quite clear. What did the Church Fathers understand the Scriptures to mean? Granted, they didn't always agree, sometimes they were silent and sometimes they even erred. However, when we read their writings we get a clear glimpse of what Christianity believed overall. This has been preserved for us today, handed down through the apostolic succession of a living Church.

Let us strive to continue in that tradition. Let us strive to share the Gospel in all generations with the deposit of faith entrusted to the Church, preserved for the world to know in the fullness of truth.

When we look at what Heaven is (from John's vision in Revelation) we see a community of saints and angels all bowing down and singing, "Holy, holy, holy" (Revelation 4:8) to the Lamb of God. You don't need to be classically trained in music. You don't need to have songs on the radio. You don't need to know how to play an instrument. You can even be completely tone-deaf! Our goal and final destination is to sing "Holy, holy, holy" before our Saviour. This is what every apologetic, every discussion, every book, and every theological discourse is meant to point us towards.

If you are struggling with "all that Catholic stuff", I invite you to go back to the beginning and read the writings of the first Christians. If that is the Church Christ established, then surely we can take comfort in returning to it.

Just like half a millennium ago, there are still many issues within the Catholic Church. There are those individuals who abuse power, who are less than ideal for the calling, who have failed and sinned. As the famous saying goes, we don't abandon Jesus (and His Church), because of the failings of Peter or even Judas. Let's be honest, we are all sinners, and we all fail. God forgive us. And despite our failings, He is still patient, loving and kind, nudging us towards deeper conversion. We are a work in progress.

The gates of Hell will not prevail against the Church Christ founded. This Church is two thousand years old, tracing its lineage in an unbroken line of succession back to the Apostles. The Catholic Church has not changed one dogma of teaching in two millennia. If this was of mere men, it would have failed long ago. It's only by the grace of God, that Christ's living Church is still standing, guarding and protecting the deposit of faith given to her by Christ Himself, handed down through the Apostles, so that in every age, all may know the fullness of truth and come to know the love of our Saviour and Messiah—Jesus. This is why we share the faith and do apologetics, with charity, gentleness and reverence. If you read nothing else, please I beg of you, read the writings of the early Church Fathers. Witness the faith that they so zealously and courageously died for.

The more we come to grow closer to the knowledge of God, the stronger our faith. The stronger our faith is, the less theological obstacles prevent us from embracing the fullness of truth that Christ desires for us. Let us strive to give an account of the hope that is in us. Let us strive to communicate that hope with the utmost gentleness, reverence and charity. Lastly, if we truly love God and others, let us strive to journey alongside those who are longing to reach the new Promised Land of Heaven, toiling and suffering with them to see them through to cross the finish line.

66 *By this everyone will know that you are my disciples, if you love one another" (John 13:35).*

ABOUT THE AUTHOR

Chris Bray is a husband to Katie and a proud father of their five daughters. He is a full-time Catholic speaker & musician. Having received multiple Gospel Music Association Covenant awards and numerous #1 hit songs on Christian radio in Canada, his ministry has spanned North America from headlining the National March for Life rally on Parliament Hill for 25,000 people, the Air Canada Centre, working with great figures such as Matt Maher, Matt Fradd, Jackie Francois, Leah Darrow, Emily Wilson, Paul J. Kim, Steve Ray, Ralph Martin, Chris Padgett, Fr. Dave Pivonka, Sr. Miriam James, Teresa Tomeo, involvement in Life Teen, World Youth Day,

Steubenville Toronto, National Catholic Youth Conference (NCYC), featured on EWTN, Salt & Light TV, 100 Huntley St., Shalom World TV, presenting to tens of thousands each year at hundreds of conferences, retreats, schools, and churches.

Learn more at www.chrisbraymusic.com

Manufactured by Amazon.ca
Bolton, ON